THE LEMON TREE

Young
Readers'
Edition

THE
LEMON
TREE

An Arab, a Jew, and
the Heart of the Middle East

SANDY TOLAN

BLOOMSBURY
CHILDREN'S BOOKS
NEW YORK LONDON OXFORD NEW DELHI SYDNEY

To Wyatt, and your sense of empathy and justice
And to his mom and my wife, Andrea Portes, with all my love

BLOOMSBURY CHILDREN'S BOOKS
Bloomsbury Publishing Inc., part of Bloomsbury Publishing Plc
1385 Broadway, New York, NY 10018

BLOOMSBURY, BLOOMSBURY CHILDREN'S BOOKS, and the Diana logo
are trademarks of Bloomsbury Publishing Plc

First published in the United States of America in October 2020
by Bloomsbury Children's Books

This edition of *The Lemon Tree* is a young readers' adaptation of
The Lemon Tree by Sandy Tolan, first published in 2006 by Bloomsbury USA.
The maps on pages viii–xii were originally published in the adult edition.

Bloomsbury Publishing Plc does not have any control over, or responsibility for, any third-party websites
referred to or in this book. All internet addresses given in this book were correct at the time of going to
press. The author and publisher regret any inconvenience caused if addresses have changed or sites have
ceased to exist, but can accept no responsibility for any such changes.

Bloomsbury books may be purchased for business or promotional use. For information on bulk purchases
please contact Macmillan Corporate and Premium Sales Department at specialmarkets@macmillan.com

Library of Congress Cataloging-in-Publication Data
Names: Tolan, Sandy, author.
Title: The lemon tree / by Sandy Tolan.
Description: [Young readers' edition]. | New York : Bloomsbury, 2020. | Adapted from the author's
adult book "The lemon tree: an Arab, a Jew, and the heart of the Middle East."
Summary: The true story of the friendship between Bashir Khairi, a Palestinian man, and
Dalia Eshkenazi Landau, an Israeli woman, whose families both had lived in the same home.
Identifiers: LCCN 2020020277 (print) | LCCN 2020020278 (e-book)
ISBN 978-1-5476-0394-7 (hardcover) • ISBN 978-1-5476-0395-4 (e-book)
Subjects: LCSH: Khayrī, Bashīr. | Landau, Dalia Eshkenazi, 1947– | Palestinian Arabs—Biography. |
Israelis—Biography. | Arab-Israeli conflict—Biography. | Ramlah (Israel)—Biography.
Classification: LCC DS126.6.K5547 T65 2020 (print) | LCC DS126.6.K5547 (e-book) |
DDC 956.9405092/2 [B]—dc23
LC record available at https://lccn.loc.gov/2020020277

Book design by John Candell
Typeset by Westchester Publishing Services
Printed and bound in the U.S.A. by Berryville Graphics Inc., Berryville, Virginia
2 4 6 8 10 9 7 5 3 1

To find out more about our authors and books visit www.bloomsbury.com and sign up for our newsletters.

CONTENTS

FIRST WORDS

*T*he house depicted in this book is an actual place, and the lemon tree in its yard is a real one. You could see the place for yourself if you boarded a bus in the West Jerusalem terminal, rode west, climbed and then plunged down the hills toward the Mediterranean, and banked up a two-lane rise until you came to a bustling, industrial town in a place once known as Palestine that is now the state of Israel. When you stepped off the bus, you'd walk down the busy main road known as Herzl Boulevard, past the juice vendors, the kebab stands, and the old storefronts selling trinkets and cheap clothing, and take a left at a street called Klausner. There, at the next corner, you'd spot a run-down gas station, and across the street a modest house with a pillared fence, a towering palm, and stones the color of cream.

This is the place, you could say to yourself. This is the house with two histories. The house with the lemon tree.

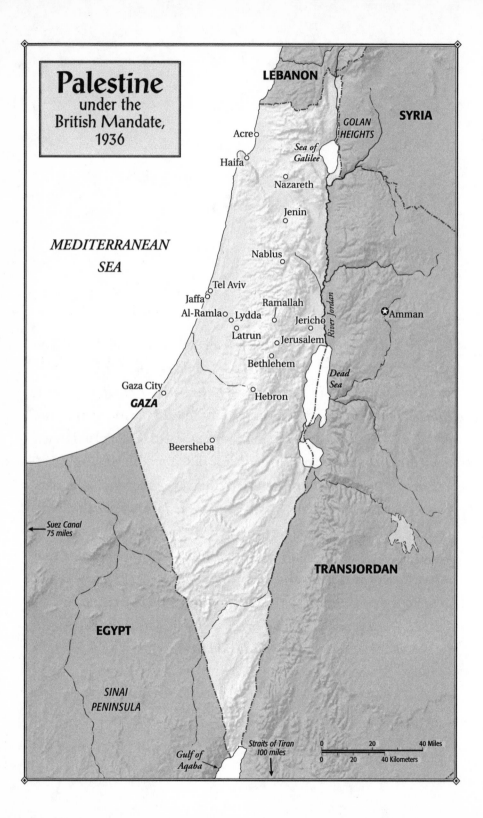

Palestine
under the British Mandate, 1936

LEBANON

SYRIA

GOLAN HEIGHTS

Acre

Sea of Galilee

Haifa

Nazareth

Jenin

MEDITERRANEAN SEA

Nablus

Tel Aviv

Jaffa

Al-Ramla

Ramallah

Lydda

Jericho

Latrun

Jerusalem

River Jordan

Amman

Bethlehem

Dead Sea

Gaza City

GAZA

Hebron

Beersheba

Suez Canal 75 miles

TRANSJORDAN

EGYPT

SINAI PENINSULA

Gulf of Aqaba

Straits of Tiran 100 miles

0	20	40 Miles
0	20	40 Kilometers

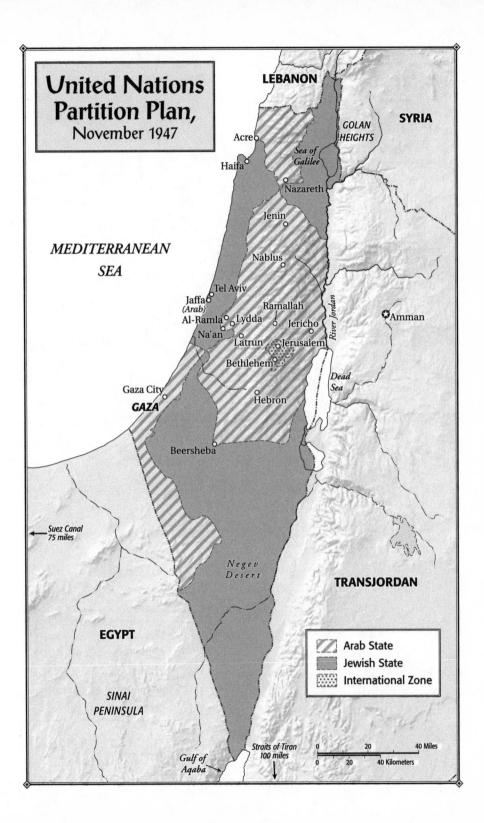

United Nations Partition Plan, November 1947

LEBANON

SYRIA

GOLAN HEIGHTS

Acre

Sea of Galilee

Haifa

Nazareth

Jenin

MEDITERRANEAN SEA

Nablus

Tel Aviv

Jaffa *(Arab)*

Ramallah

Al-Ramla

Lydda

Jericho

Na'an

Latrun

Jerusalem

Bethlehem

River Jordan

Amman

Dead Sea

Gaza City

GAZA

Hebron

Beersheba

Suez Canal 75 miles

Negev Desert

TRANSJORDAN

EGYPT

SINAI PENINSULA

Gulf of Aqaba

Straits of Tiran 100 miles

Arab State	
Jewish State	
International Zone	

0   20   40 Miles

0   20   40 Kilometers

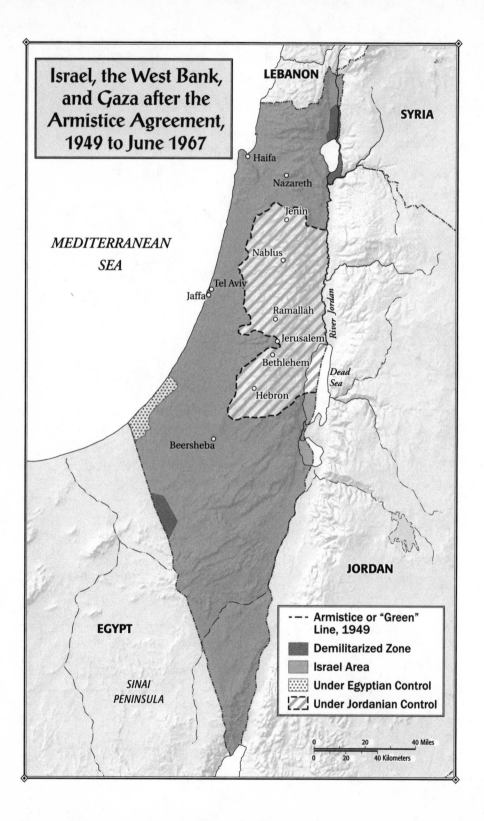

Israel, the West Bank,
and Gaza after the
Armistice Agreement,
1949 to June 1967

LEBANON

SYRIA

MEDITERRANEAN
SEA

Haifa

Nazareth

Jenin

Nablus

Tel Aviv
Jaffa

Ramallah

Jerusalem

Bethlehem

Hebron

Beersheba

River Jordan

Dead
Sea

JORDAN

EGYPT

SINAI
PENINSULA

- - - Armistice or "Green"
Line, 1949

Demilitarized Zone

Israel Area

Under Egyptian Control

Under Jordanian Control

0   20   40 Miles

0   20   40 Kilometers

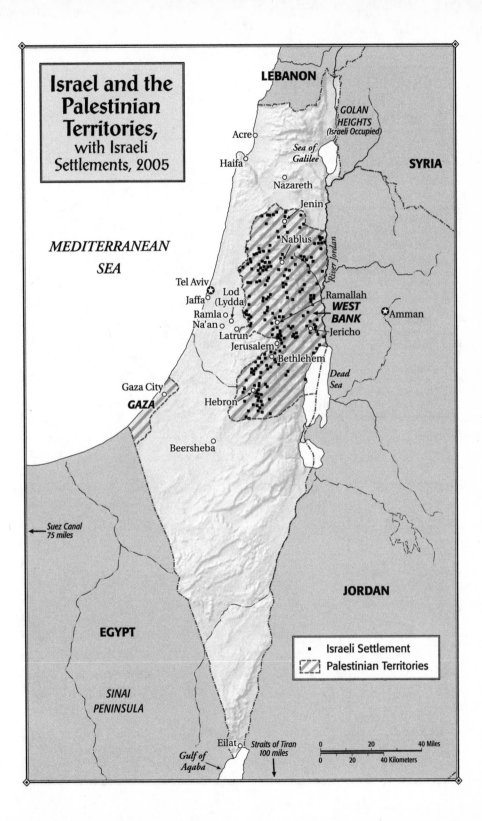

Israel and the Palestinian Territories, with Israeli Settlements, 2005

LEBANON

GOLAN HEIGHTS
(Israeli Occupied)

SYRIA

Acre

Sea of Galilee

Haifa

Nazareth

Jenin

Nablus

MEDITERRANEAN SEA

River Jordan

Tel Aviv
Jaffa
Lod (Lydda)
Ramla
Na'an
Latrun
Jerusalem
Bethlehem

Ramallah
WEST BANK
Jericho

Amman

Dead Sea

Gaza City
GAZA
Hebron

Beersheba

Suez Canal 75 miles ←

JORDAN

EGYPT

SINAI PENINSULA

Eilat
Straits of Tiran 100 miles ↓

Gulf of Aqaba

| • | Israeli Settlement |
| ▨ | Palestinian Territories |

0   20   40 Miles
0   20   40 Kilometers

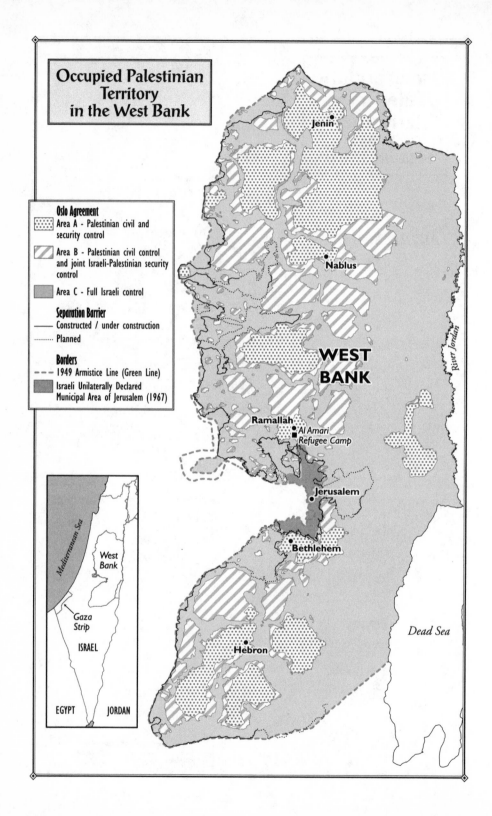

Occupied Palestinian Territory in the West Bank

Oslo Agreement
- Area A - Palestinian civil and security control
- Area B - Palestinian civil control and joint Israeli-Palestinian security control
- Area C - Full Israeli control

Separation Barrier
- —— Constructed / under construction
- ·········· Planned

Borders
- --- 1949 Armistice Line (Green Line)
- Israeli Unilaterally Declared Municipal Area of Jerusalem (1967)

Jenin

Nablus

WEST BANK

River Jordan

Ramallah

Al Amari Refugee Camp

Jerusalem

Bethlehem

Dead Sea

Hebron

Mediterranean Sea

West Bank

Gaza Strip

ISRAEL

EGYPT   JORDAN

INTRODUCTION

In early 1998, I set out for Israel and the West Bank in search of a surprisingly elusive story. Despite the forests' worth of newspapers and miles of videotape documenting the seemingly endless conflict between Israelis and Palestinians, I found very little about the human side of the story, the common ground between enemies, and genuine hopes that two peoples can live in equality and mutual respect on the same land. My assignment came on the eve of the fiftieth anniversary of the first Arab-Israeli war, in 1948—known as the "War of Independence" in Israel, and to Palestinians as the "Nakba," or Catastrophe. I wanted to explore how this event, and the history that followed it, was understood by ordinary people—Palestinians and Israelis living in the Holy Land. I needed to find two families linked by history in a tangible way.

I spent weeks reading Israeli military history, Palestinian oral history, and scholarly works, looking at the roots of the conflict. I traveled from Jerusalem to Tel Aviv, from Ramallah to Hebron to Gaza, digging for the human story that would move beyond the heartbreaking images transmitted from the region.

I encountered many dead ends. But then I came across something real. It was the true story of one house, two families, and a common history emanating from walls of Jerusalem stone on the coastal plain east of Tel Aviv and Jaffa. From a single house, and the lemon tree in its garden, lay a path to the histories, both separate and intertwined, of two families, the Khairis and the Eshkenazis, and to the larger story of two peoples on one land. Their family histories allowed me to go beyond the familiar story of pain and retaliation. As I began interviews with Bashir Khairi in Ramallah and Dalia Eshkenazi Landau in Jerusalem, I quickly saw that I would cross new landscape, to the twin hearts of the story.

Like many Americans, I grew up with one part of the history, as told through the heroic birth of Israel out of the Holocaust. The mother of one of my schoolmates had lived in Anne Frank's neighborhood, even played marbles with Anne Frank as a child. Her family escaped on a ship from Amsterdam, just in time, before the Nazis arrived. I knew of Israel as a safe haven for the Jews. I knew nothing about the Arab side. For millions of Americans, Jew and Gentile, it was the same. They too were raised with the version of Middle Eastern history as told in *Exodus,* Leon Uris's hugely influential megabestseller, later made into a movie starring legendary actor Paul Newman. In Uris's engaging novel, Palestinians are alternately pathetic or malicious, or perhaps worse—they have no real claim to the land: "If the Arabs of Palestine loved their land, they could not have been forced from it—much less run from it without real cause." But as generations of historians have since documented, and as Dalia and Bashir recounted to me in their own words, the actual history of the two people's relations is far more complex, not to mention richer and a lot more interesting.

The Lemon Tree—the book you're holding—is entirely a work of nonfiction. In other words, I didn't make anything up! While many of the events described here happened decades ago, their retelling is based on hundreds of interviews, documents from historical archives, published and unpublished memoirs, newspaper clippings, radio and television recordings, and many other historical accounts. For this book, I conducted interviews in Israel, the West Bank, Jordan, Lebanon, and Bulgaria over a period of seven years. I visited archives in Jerusalem, Ramallah, Beirut, Sofia (the capital of Bulgaria), London, New York, and Austin, Texas.

I first told the story of Dalia and Bashir in a documentary broadcast on the NPR program *Fresh Air* in May 1998, on the anniversary of the first day of the 1948 War (or the Nakba, or the War of Independence).

But a radio program is one thing; a book rich with family stories and decades of history is something else completely. My challenge was to keep the two people and families, one Palestinian and one Israeli, at the center of the book. I wanted to write a history book in disguise, and to make it feel, throughout, like a good novel.

Even though the story is true.

Chapter 1
BASHIR

Bashir Khairi approached a mirror in the washroom of Israel's West Jerusalem bus station. The young Arab man stood alone before a row of porcelain basins and leaned forward, studying himself. He turned his head slightly, left to right and back again. He smoothed his hair, nudged his tie, and pinched his clean-shaven face. He was making certain that all of this was real.

For nearly two decades—since he was six years old—Bashir had been planning for this journey. It was the breath, the currency, the bread of his family, of every family he knew. It was what everyone talked about, all the time: return. In exile, there was little else worth dreaming about.

Bashir gazed at his reflection. *Are you ready for this journey?* he asked himself. *Are you worthy of it?* It seemed his destiny to return to the place he'd mainly only heard about and mostly couldn't remember. It felt as if he were being drawn back by hidden magic, as if he were preparing to meet a secret, long-lost partner. He wanted to look good.

"Bashir!" yelled his cousin Yasser, snapping the younger man back to the moment in the bus station men's room. "Yallah! Come on! The bus is leaving!"

The two men walked into the large waiting hall of the terminal, where their cousin Ghiath was waiting.

It was almost noon on a hot day in July 1967. All around Bashir, Yasser, and Ghiath, strangers rushed past: Israeli women in white blouses and long, dark skirts; men in wide-brimmed black hats and white beards; and children with sidelocks. The cousins hurried toward their bus.

They had come that morning from Ramallah, a Palestinian hill town half an hour to the north, where they lived as refugees. Before they left, the cousins had asked their friends and neighbors how to navigate this alien world called Israel: Which bus should we take? How much does a ticket cost? How do we buy it? Will anyone check our papers once we board the bus? What will they do if they find out we are Palestinians?

Bashir and his cousins had left Ramallah in the late morning. They rode south in a group taxi to East Jerusalem and arrived at the walls of the Old City, the end of the first leg of their journey. Only weeks before, those walls had been the site of fierce combat, leading to devastation for the Arabs and the occupation of East Jerusalem by Israel. Emerging from the taxi, the cousins could see soldiers stationed at Damascus Gate, the northern entrance to the Old City. From there the three men turned west and walked away from the ancient walls.

They crossed an invisible line.

The line was the boundary between two nations. Until a few weeks before, the line had divided West Jerusalem and Israel from Arab East Jerusalem and the West Bank. Now, after the defeat of the Arabs in the Six-Day War, Israeli forces occupied the West Bank, the Sinai

Peninsula, and the Golan Heights and were defending the new frontiers.

Bashir and his cousins had found it easy to cross into a territory both old and new. They'd trudged in the heat for several miles, down crowded lanes and past stone houses that seemed vaguely familiar. Finally, the narrow streets had given way to busy, modern avenues, where the West Jerusalem bus station had come into view.

The young men hurried across the concrete terminal floor, past the station agents pushing tickets through metal bars, past the kiosk selling candies, gum, and newspapers in a language they could not recognize. On the platforms at the far end of the terminal stood buses bound for lands they had only heard about: the forests in the north; the southern desert; the coastal plain. Bashir and his cousins held their tickets to al-Ramla and hurried toward platform 10, where their bus—painted in waves of aqua and white—was ready to take them home.

With a low rumble and a burst of exhaust, the bus began to descend the hills west of Jerusalem, taking the three cousins toward their hometown. They had boarded the bus with a prior agreement not to sit together. This would eliminate the temptation to speak to one another, thus reducing any suspicion among the other passengers about their identity. By sitting apart, each cousin could also have a window seat, to take in every inch of the journey home. They sat one behind the other, absorbing the scenery.

Bashir wasn't sure if he wanted the trip to go quickly or slowly. If it went quickly, he would be in al-Ramla sooner, but if time slowed down, he could more fully take in each bend, each landmark, each piece of his own history.

The bus roared up the curving highway toward the crest of the famous hilltop at Qastal. Here, a great Arab commander had fallen in battle nineteen years earlier, breaking the back of his people's army and opening the road to the Holy City for the enemy. Beyond the hilltop, Bashir could see the stone minarets of the mosque at Abu Ghosh, one of the few Arab villages that remained standing on the road between Jerusalem and the sea. The village leaders there had collaborated with the enemy, and their village had been spared. Bashir looked upon the mosque's minarets with mixed feelings.

The bus sped down the hillside, easing up as the mountain walls closed in and then opened to a broad valley below. Eight centuries earlier, Bashir's Arab ancestors had battled Christian invaders in hand-to-hand combat, repelling them for a time. Along the roadside, Bashir saw burned carcasses of vehicles blown up nineteen years earlier, in the more recent war, and wreaths and fading flowers laid alongside them. The Israelis who had placed these wreaths were honoring what they called their War of Independence. To Bashir, this same event was known as the Nakba, or "Catastrophe."

In the valley, they passed irrigated wheat fields and angled up a low rise. Near the village of Latrun, Bashir suddenly recalled a journey made in haste and fear nearly two decades before. The details were hard to remember, since they were from events that happened when he was six years old—events he had brooded about nearly every day for the past nineteen years.

Bashir glanced at the Israeli man seated next him, who was absorbed in a book. Looking out the window meant nothing to this man, Bashir thought. Perhaps he'd seen the view many times already. Decades later, Bashir would recall feeling jealous of the man's inattention to the landscape.

The bus hit a bump—it was the railroad crossing. Simultaneously, the three cousins experienced a familiar sensation, grooved into their memories by a repetition from nineteen years before.

Bashir and his cousins knew they had arrived in al-Ramla.

They emerged from the bus into a hot, glaring world that seemed both bizarre and familiar. Bashir could see the old municipality building, and the town cinema, and the edge of the neighborhood where he and his cousins had been raised. But none of the streets seemed familiar, at least not at first: they all had new names. Most of the old buildings were covered with brightly colored signs in blocky Hebrew lettering. On some of the buildings' archways, remnants of the original flowing, cursive Arabic letters remained.

Yasser, the oldest, spotted something he knew: the old neighborhood butcher's shop. He hurried inside with his cousins following, and threw his arms around the butcher, kissing both his cheeks in the customary way of the Arabs. "Abu Muhammad," he shouted.

The Jewish butcher couldn't have been more startled. Abu Muhammad had left many years before. The new butcher's name was Mordechai. He invited the cousins to stay for kebab, but they were too stunned by the butcher's true identity and too distracted by their mission to accept his offer of food. They walked out, flustered.

"You were pretending you know everything here," Ghiath teased Yasser. "You don't know anything here."

The cousins turned a corner and found themselves in the quieter streets of the neighborhood where they once played. They felt at ease and happy, and they forgot their earlier concern about speaking to one another. They spoke openly in their mother tongue.

They approached the door of Yasser's house, and he stepped forward to knock. A woman came out, looking at them strangely.

"Please," Yasser said, "all we want is to see the house we lived in before."

The woman grew agitated. "If you don't leave, I will call the police!" she screamed. The cousins tried to calm her, explaining their purpose. The woman continued shouting, taking a step forward and shoving them back. Neighbors began opening their doors. Eventually the cousins realized they might soon find themselves in trouble with the local authorities, and they hurried away.

Yasser drifted along in a silent daze. "It was as if he had no soul," Bashir later recalled. "He was a walking body, nothing more."

"I cannot accept such a feeling," Yasser said finally. "It is something that I cannot bear."

Soon they came to the house where Ghiath had grown up. Outside was a large sign they couldn't read and a guard armed with a machine gun. The two-story house was now a school. The guard told the young men to wait while he went inside. A moment later the principal came out and invited them in for tea. She told them they could walk through the rooms when the class period ended, and she left them in her office to wait.

They silently sipped their tea. Ghiath removed his glasses and wiped his eyes. He put them back on and tried to look cheerful. "I can't control my feelings," he whispered.

"I know," Bashir said quietly. "I understand."

When the principal returned, she invited them to tour the house. They did so. Ghiath cried the whole time.

After their visit, they walked in the direction of Bashir's old home. No one could remember exactly where it was. Bashir recalled that it had both a front door, and a back door that faced a side street. It had a front gate with a bell, a flowering *fitna* tree in the front yard, and a lemon tree in the back. After walking in circles in the heat, Bashir realized he'd found the house. He heard a voice from somewhere deep inside himself: *This is your home.*

Bashir and his cousins approached the house. Everything depended on the reception, Bashir told himself. He couldn't know what the outcome would be, especially after what had happened to Yasser. "It all depends," he said, "on who is on the other side of the door."

Chapter 2
DALIA

On that same July day, Dalia Eshkenazi sat alone at the kitchen table of the only home she had ever known. Sunlight streamed in through the south-facing windows of the stone house as she sipped her tea and ate black bread spread thick with Bulgarian cheese.

Dalia had no special plans for the day. She could catch up on her summer reading for the university, where she studied English literature. Or she could look contentedly into the depths of the jacaranda tree, as she'd done countless times before.

In recent days, life in Dalia's home and her hometown of Ramla had returned to normal—as normal as could be expected, at least, in the Israel of 1967. The air raids had ended, and Dalia's parents were back at work. The young woman had time to ponder her emotions of the past few months.

First had been the unbearable tension and the trauma before the six days of war. Unfamiliar voices broadcasting from Cairo told her people to go back where they came from or be pushed into the sea. Some Israelis thought the threats were funny, but for Dalia, whose family had been through the Holocaust, it was impossible to fully express the depths of fear those threats awakened.

For a month before the war, Dalia had felt that the end was coming. "Not just the disintegration of the state, but the end of us as a people," she remembered. Alongside this fear was a determination, born from the Holocaust, "to never again be led like sheep to the slaughter."

Late on the first night of the Six-Day War, Dalia learned that Israel had destroyed the enemy's air force. She knew then that the outcome of the war was essentially decided. Dalia believed that God had had a hand in Israel's survival and compared her own feeling of awe and wonder with the feeling she imagined her Jewish ancestors had had when witnessing the parting of the Red Sea.

Dalia's parents had grown up in Bulgaria, married in 1940, survived Bulgaria's pro-Nazi government, and moved to Israel after World War II. Dalia was eleven months old when she arrived.

Dalia's family had been spared the atrocities in Bulgaria by acts of goodwill from Christians she was raised to admire and remember. Now, she believed her people had a destiny to live on the land of Israel. This was partly why she believed what she had been told: the Arabs who had lived in this house, and in hundreds of other stone homes in her city, had simply run away.

Dalia rinsed her morning dishes, wiped her hands on a towel, and walked to the kitchen doorway, which opened onto the garden. In recent days, she'd been carrying on a silent dialogue with God that she began as a child. *Why,* she thought, *would You allow Israel to be saved during the Six-Day War, yet not prevent genocide during the Holocaust? Why would you empower Israel's warriors to vanquish its enemies, yet stand by while my people were branded and slaughtered a generation earlier?*

For a child, it was difficult to comprehend the trauma of the people who surrounded her, who had been through World War II and the Holocaust. Only after probing could Dalia begin to understand. She had asked her mother some of the particulars: How were the people branded by the Nazis? Did they stand in line at the concentration camps? Did branding hurt? Why would anyone do these things? Over the years, Dalia's curiosity helped her understand the silence of the children she had grown up with—children she would invite home after school and try to cheer up with her elaborate skits and solo performances in the garden.

Through the doorway, Dalia looked out at the jacaranda tree her father had planted amid the flower beds. As a girl, Dalia had loved to water the deep red Queen Elizabeth roses, with their overwhelming perfume.

Near the jacaranda tree stood the lemon tree. Another family had planted that tree; it was already bearing fruit when Dalia and her parents arrived nearly nineteen years earlier. Dalia was aware she'd grown up in an Arab home, and sometimes she wondered about the previous residents. Had children lived here? How many? How old were they then? In school Dalia had been taught that the Arabs fled like cowards, with their hot soup still steaming on the table. As a younger child, she hadn't questioned this story, but the older she got, the less sense it made. Why would anyone voluntarily leave such a beautiful house? At that same moment, Bashir and his cousins approached the metal gate in front of the house. Bashir reached for the bell, and pressed it.

Chapter 3
THE HOUSE

Ahmad Khairi built the house for his family in 1936. The stone—pockmarked and rough, the color of cream—was cut in foot-thick slabs. Its dips and rises looked like a miniature landscape, like the hills and wadis of Palestine.

Ahmad stood in an open field in his coat and tie and Turkish fez. He crouched low and laid the first stone on its foundation. Hundreds of other chiseled slabs of white Jerusalem stone were stacked high behind him. With the first stone in place, Ahmad's cousins, friends, and hired laborers began to place stone upon mortar upon stone.

The house would stand at the eastern edge of al-Ramla, an Arab town on the coastal plain between Jerusalem and the Mediterranean Sea. The nearby Palestinian farms produced abundant crops of barley, wheat, cabbages, cucumbers, tomatoes, figs, grapes, and melons.

The Khairis had been in the region for several hundred years, living in an expanse of open grounds and houses connected by stone gates and archways. They tended oranges, olives, and almonds, and their land was administered under Islamic law. The Khairis usually married within their clan, but Ahmad was an exception. Seven years earlier, he'd married a nineteen-year-old woman named Zakia, from the Riad family of al-Ramla. She was much loved by the Khairis.

Ahmad watched as the walls of his house rose with fourteen layers of Jerusalem stone. His decision to move out of the family compound was unusual. He wanted some independence. Ahmad's uncle Sheikh Mustafa Khairi agreed, since Ahmad had an inheritance and a successful furniture business as well as a growing family—Zakia was pregnant with the couple's fourth child.

Ahmad and a Jewish friend and architect, Benson Solli, had designed the house with large living and sleeping quarters separated by double wooden doors. There would be an inside kitchen for Zakia, and indoor plumbing. These were new luxuries in a town that was founded twelve centuries earlier.

The workers hung wooden shutters on the windows and laid tiles for a small garage. Before long, Ahmad turned his attention to the garden. In the corner of the yard behind the house, he'd chosen a spot for a lemon tree. Once the tree was in the soil, Ahmad knew it would be at least seven years before the strong Palestinian sun and the sweet waters of the al-Ramla aquifer would nurture it to maturity. So planting the tree was an act of faith and patience.

The house was finished by late 1936. To celebrate, the family butchered a lamb and prepared a huge feast: chicken stuffed with rice and great piles of lamb were common for such occasions, along with homemade couscous; date-filled cookies made with soft, buttery dough; and kanafe, a hot, pistachio-covered sweet that's shaped like a pizza and looks like shredded wheat.

Cousins, sisters, and brothers came from the Khairi family compound to admire the new home. So did Sheikh Mustafa, who had raised Ahmad like a son.

There stood Ahmad, in his coat and tie and fez; a pregnant Zakia; and their three girls, Hiam, Basima, and Fatima.

The sense of security the Khairis might have hoped for in the new home—on land their families had inhabited for centuries—was tempered by the reality of daily life in Palestine. Their homeland was in the midst of a full-scale rebellion.

Al-Ramla, and all of Palestine, had been ruled by the British since 1917, just before the end of World War I. That year, the British had pledged to help establish a "national homeland for Jewish people" in Palestine. That pledge was a triumph for Zionism, a political movement of European Jews. The British planned to develop public works, utilities, and natural resources, laying the foundation for a Jewish government in Palestine. In the years since, Jewish people had begun moving to the area, causing tension between the Arabs and the British.

As the longtime mayor of al-Ramla, Sheikh Mustafa Khairi often helped settle disputes between the British overseers and his restive fellow Palestinians. But for the Khairis, as for many Arabs, the Jews had always been part of Palestine. They bartered with one another for wheat, barley, and melons at al-Ramla's market, and people from both groups worked as engineers and conductors for the Palestine railroad that passed through town. Arab laborers worked in nearby Jewish fields, and Jewish farmers brought their horses into al-Ramla to be shod.

Wealthy Arab residents of al-Ramla traveled to the city of Tel Aviv to have their suits cut by Jewish tailors, their fezzes cleaned by Jewish dry cleaners, or their portraits taken by Jewish photographers. At the school attended by Ahmad and Zakia's daughters, many of the girls' classmates were Jews. "They all spoke Arabic and were

Palestinians like us," one of the daughters recalled decades later. "They were there—like us, part of Palestine."

But by 1936, as Ahmad's house rose, the harmony had begun to disintegrate.

Adolf Hitler had taken power in Germany three years earlier, and now the situation for Jews was deteriorating across Europe. Demands for Jewish immigration to Palestine increased. Underground Zionist organizations began smuggling boatloads of Jews from European ports to Haifa, on the Mediterranean coast of Palestine. The Jewish population of the region grew rapidly, and Arabs began to fear Jewish domination. Soon Arab leaders declared that selling land to the Jews was an act of treason. They opposed a separate Jewish state, and they wanted the British out of Palestine.

The Great Arab Rebellion had erupted the previous fall when a band of rebels took to the hills. Arab nationalists had long suspected the British of favoring Jews over the Arabs in Palestine. The British claimed that efforts to build a Jewish state would not adversely affect "the civil and religious rights of existing non-Jewish communities in Palestine." But the leader of the Arab Rebellion was convinced that only an armed uprising could bring about national liberation for the Arabs.

The British accused the rebels of causing two firebomb deaths in a Jewish community, or kibbutz. They called the rebel leader a terrorist, and he was hunted down and killed. More violence followed, with both Jewish and Arab people killed, stores robbed, kibbutzes fired on, and trains derailed.

Amid the conflict, Zakia gave birth to a fourth daughter, Khanom. Ahmad's furniture business continued to thrive despite the ongoing Arab Rebellion. In the evenings he would join the other Khairi men to play cards and drink Arabic coffee at the social gathering place in the family compound. There the talk of politics was unending.

In July 1937, a British committee recommended that Palestine be divided into two states—one for Jews and one for Arabs. Hundreds of Arab villages were within the proposed boundaries of the new Jewish state, while more than a thousand Jews resided on the Arab side of the partition line. The committee stated that an "arrangement" would have to be made "for the transfer, voluntary or otherwise, of land and population . . ."

The Zionist leaders accepted the recommendations, though not all agreed. Many Jewish leaders did not want to give up the idea of a Jewish homeland across all of Palestine.

Arabs were stunned by the proposal. The Arab Higher Committee promptly rejected it, not only because of the transfer plan, but also because of the partition itself. The Arabs would fight for a single, independent, Arab-majority state.

The Arab Rebellion erupted again a few months later when a British commissioner was killed by Arab assassins. The British response was swift. The military took control from civil authorities, and military courts stepped up executions of suspected rebels. Thousands of Arabs were jailed as British troops occupied cities and towns across Palestine, including al-Ramla.

Sheikh Mustafa Khairi hoped to maintain peace, but he was caught between the British forces and the leaders of the Arab Rebellion. For fifteen years, he had commanded great respect as al-Ramla's mayor and the leader of one of its most influential families. His popularity was based on his defense of the rural poor.

Now Mustafa Khairi was a mayor in a land under foreign occupation, and he needed to cooperate with the British authorities. For a time he stood up to rebel leaders who demanded taxes to fuel the Arab Rebellion. But in 1938 he briefly fled to Cairo due to fears that he would be assassinated.

Fighting continued, and conflicting political decisions by the British authorities angered both Arabs and Jews. By 1940, the Arab Rebellion had been defeated through "severe countermeasures": tens of thousands jailed, thousands killed, hundreds executed, countless houses demolished, and key leaders in exile.

The Palestinian national movement was deeply divided and utterly unprepared for any future conflict. A lull in the battle for the future of Palestine restored some sense of order, and Mayor Khairi went back to attending to his municipal duties, confronting black marketers who were illegally hoarding food to get around wartime rationing, and dealing with a failed well and a shortage of water in the town.

On February 2, 1942, the mayor was distracted by something far more pleasant than water troubles, political attacks, and the prospect of fresh violence in Palestine. His nephew Ahmad became a father for the seventh time. Zakia gave birth to their first boy. He was born at home, with the help of a midwife.

Relatives came from Gaza, and the entire Khairi clan celebrated with song and dance.

They called the child Bashir.

Chapter 4
BULGARIA

As World War II raged and Hitler's power spread across Europe, Jews were being rounded up, sent to concentration camps, and exterminated. In Bulgaria, none of this had happened yet, but Moshe and Solia, with their infant daughter Dalia, began feeling great unease.

By early 1943 Bulgaria was aligned with the Axis powers (Germany, Italy, and Japan), and terrible stories from elsewhere in Europe were drifting over the borders. Bulgaria's forty-seven thousand Jews had lost many of their rights and felt increasingly unsettled. On a frigid morning in March of that year, Moshe and Solia Eshkenazi received a letter instructing them to pack twenty kilograms of food and clothing and prepare for a journey. Years later, Solia vividly recalled her fear to her daughter, Dalia: *This is the end.*

Hundreds of Bulgarian Jews received similar orders, and it appeared that their fate was to be identical to that of the rest of European Jewry. That path had seemed clear for at least two years, since the imposition of anti-Jewish laws and the country's alliance with Hitler.

But many Bulgarians stood by their Jewish neighbors. Word of the

massive deportations had been leaked by concerned government officials, leading to protests; Bulgaria's top religious officials also spoke
out against the plan. And instead of forty-seven thousand Bulgarian
Jews being sent to their deaths in gas chambers, nearly all were
spared. The history of Bulgarian Jewry is therefore unlike any other
across Europe.

Some European Jews had already departed for Palestine, but for
Solia and Moshe the prospect of emigration seemed remote. Their
families lived here; their work was here. Even after the threats of 1943,
they were still Bulgarian. But the country was suffering from the
effects of World War II.

Bulgaria was a devastated landscape. American bombings in late
1943 and early 1944 had flattened much of the capital city of Sofia,
including the parliament building. The relentless blitzes killed many
and drove residents into the countryside. Villages were overrun with
refugees. Crop failures brought food shortages and hunger, and run-
away inflation deepened the crisis. By the late fall of 1944, the country's new, impoverished communist government had begun to look
beyond its borders for help.

David Ben-Gurion, the leader of the Zionists in Palestine, visited
Sofia with a plan. He was received by government and religious leaders. Ben-Gurion's goal was to win an agreement to allow Bulgarian
Jews to emigrate to Palestine. Rehabilitating the Jews of Bulgaria
would be impossible, he told the officials; they had to be permitted
to leave. Establishing a Jewish state in Palestine was "the task of the
moment."

Ben-Gurion had a strategy. He knew that Bulgaria was in desperate need of cash and basic goods. He was shocked by the devastation
and poverty he'd witnessed in and around Sofia, and he arranged for

temporary aid for the nation's Jews, with a long-term goal of bringing them to a new Jewish state.

He had five thousand pairs of children's shoes shipped to Bulgaria for Jewish children, but he remarked, "Maybe it is a better idea if we try to bring the feet to the shoes." By the end of 1944, more than 1,300 Jews had left Bulgaria for Palestine, including one of Solia's cousins.

Before long, the Jewish Agency in Palestine opened trade relations with the new Bulgarian government.

Young people like Moshe and Solia became intrigued by talk of a new life in Palestine. Others preferred to rebuild the Jewish community in Bulgaria and viewed the Zionists as "reactionaries" who didn't "believe in the Fatherland Front"—the country's ruling communist party.

For Moshe and Solia, the decision to stay or to leave remained a difficult one. The promise of Palestine had to be weighed against the prospect of rebuilding their lives with friends and family in Bulgaria.

Moshe worked to reestablish himself as a salesman of fine clothing, and he and Solia began planning for a family. But communism brought collectives and cooperatives, which replaced grocers, craftsmen, and merchants. Moshe, Solia, and other Jewish families whose modest incomes relied on private enterprise now had another factor weighing in favor of emigration.

In the spring of 1947, the Soviet ambassador to the United Nations stunned Zionists by suggesting that the Soviet Union would support a Jewish state in Palestine. Shortly after, the Soviets gave additional details: they would join the United States in supporting a UN plan to partition Palestine into separate Arab and Jewish states. Celebrations broke out in Jewish communities throughout Bulgaria.

Around that same time, Solia became pregnant. On a cold December evening in 1947, she gave birth to a daughter.

"There is a girl, and her name is Daizy!" Moshe exclaimed. (Daizy later changed her name to Dalia.)

The couple had wanted a child throughout their seven years of marriage; they had even hoped for a girl. Now they had to decide where she would grow up.

Chapter 5
DIVISION

Ten days after the birth of their first son, in February 1942, Ahmad and Zakia, their infant boy, his sisters, his great-uncle Sheikh Mustafa, and several dozen cousins, aunts, and uncles were packed into buses riding southeast on the narrow roads of Palestine. They rolled past the watermelon fields of Na'ani, just south of al-Ramla; past the cool, sweet springs of Imwas; past the stone minaret of Deir Aban, home of the finest wheat in all Palestine; past olive groves and sloping, rain-fed fields and into al-Khalil, or Hebron, where the imam was waiting at the mosque.

"A name should be prescribed for the child," the prophet Mohammad had observed. "Its hair and all filth should be removed, and sacrifice should be performed on his behalf."

At the ceremony inside the Mosque of Abraham, the patriarch of three great faiths, the imam spoke the baby's name: Bashir, Arabic for "good news" or "the bearer of good tidings."

His hair was cut and weighed; the family would give to the poor the value of that weight in gold. Sheep were slaughtered, and two-thirds of the meat would be given to the poor. The clan had a feast with the rest.

Back in al-Ramla, schoolteachers congratulated the Khairi girls on the arrival of their baby brother. At home, the girls doted on Bashir. As a toddler he would stand on a table, dressed in white trousers and white shoes, making impromptu speeches to his adoring older sisters. "He was handsome," his sister Nuha recalled. "Like King Farouk," the ruler of Egypt.

By then, Sheikh Mustafa Khairi had been mayor of al-Ramla for more than twenty years, and the tension of nationalist politics had given way to the headaches of rations and rising prices under British wartime rule. But the war economy had helped much of Palestine. The British used the territory as a massive staging area for the conflict in North Africa. Smooth asphalt roads began to replace the rutted dirt tracks of old Palestine. Work was plentiful, and Ahmad's furniture business was faring well.

In Africa and Europe, World War II had turned toward the Allies. Soviet troops had defeated the Nazis in the battle of Stalingrad. Closer to Palestine, British troops, aided by many Jewish recruits, had triumphed in North Africa and eliminated the prospect of a Nazi march toward Tel Aviv and Jerusalem.

By the end of the war, in 1945, Bashir had turned three and the battle for the future of Palestine had reawakened. A quarter of a million Jewish refugees flooded Allied displaced-persons camps in Europe, and tens of thousands of Jews were smuggled out of those camps to Palestine by the Mossad, the predecessor of Israel's present-day spy agency. Most of this immigration was illegal under the British rule of Palestine, and British authorities began to intercept boatloads of European Jews and intern them on the Mediterranean island of Cyprus. Several years earlier, the British had imposed strict immigration limits in the face of the fears, demands, and rebellion of the Palestinian Arabs.

As details of the atrocities in Europe began to emerge, however, images of stateless, bedraggled Holocaust survivors in the Cyprus camps were seared into the minds of the Western public, and Britain was pressured to loosen its policy. U.S. president Harry Truman urged Britain to allow one hundred thousand displaced persons into Palestine as soon as possible and to abandon restrictions on land sales to Jews. Both measures were certain to increase tensions with the Arabs of Palestine.

Arabs argued that the Holocaust survivors could be settled elsewhere, including in the United States, which had imposed its own limits on the settlement of European Jews, and refused to loosen them. The Zionists were intent on settling the refugees in Palestine, however, not anywhere else. But in early 1947, when the ship *Exodus* arrived in Palestine's Haifa port, British authorities denied entry to the 4,500 Jewish refugees, forcing them to board other ships and return to Germany. A French newspaper called the *Exodus* a "floating Auschwitz." The incident shocked the Western world and deepened support for the Zionist movement.

The earlier cooperation between the British Empire and the Zionists had all but vanished. The Jewish Agency had been authorized by the British to create "a national home for the Jewish people." Now, nearly three decades later, the Jewish community in Palestine had grown into a powerful economic and political force. It even had its own militia—the Haganah—in addition to extremist groups, which fought to expel the British. Bombs planted by one of those groups exploded in Jerusalem's King David Hotel, where the British housed their military and intelligence headquarters, killing more than eighty people. Tensions escalated between the Haganah, controlled by David Ben-Gurion, and the Jewish extremist groups—Irgun, led by Menachem Begin, and the Stern Gang, led by Yitzhak Shamir. Both men would later become prime ministers of Israel.

Britain still had eighty-four thousand soldiers in Palestine, but the British Colonial Office reported that they "received no cooperation from the Jewish community."

In fact, the Jewish militias had attacked communications systems, trains, and government buildings. A report by the British Colonial Office declared that British troops "had proved insufficient to maintain law and order in the face of a campaign of terrorism waged by highly organized Jewish forces equipped with all the weapons of the modern infantryman."

Meanwhile, British officials were under pressure at home to convert factories and revive the postwar economy. In February, the government announced that it would hand over the problem of Palestine to the newly formed United Nations, which planned to send a fact-finding team to investigate the roots of the struggle for Palestine.

That same month, Bashir turned five. He was shy, frightened of dogs and strangers. He liked to sit inside with his sister Nuha, gazing out the window at the railroad tracks for hours at a time as they waited to see the Jaffa-to-Jerusalem train.

On their way to school, looking crisp in their matching uniforms, the Khairi children would notice the British soldiers in their khaki shorts and soft brown hats. The older girls began to understand the political context of the soldiers' presence. A teacher told them about the growing threat to their homeland.

By the fall of 1947, nearly everyone in Palestine was anxious about the UN investigation and how its recommendations could determine their future. There was talk about a division of Palestine into separate states for Arabs and Jews. Most Palestinian Arabs saw that as a catastrophe; they wanted one Palestine.

Ahmad increasingly found his discussions over coffee at the family compound turning to the sorry state of the Palestinian Arab leadership. The Arabs were weaker and more fractured than ever. Thousands of men had been killed or wounded during the Arab Rebellion and tens of thousands imprisoned. The leader of the rebels— Hajj Amin al-Husseini—was in exile, and his image was permanently tainted in the West after he'd taken up with the Nazis. But many Arabs in Palestine still viewed him as a hero who could deliver an independent state across all of Palestine.

In November the UN General Assembly voted to partition Palestine into two separate states—one for the Arabs and one for the Jews. (A second proposal, which recommended a single state for Arabs and Jews, with a constitution respecting "human rights and fundamental freedoms without distinction as to race, sex, language or religions," was rejected.)

Palestine was to be divided. After three decades of colonial rule, the British would leave on May 15, 1948. If all went according to plan, the Arab and Jewish states would be born on the same day.

The Khairis were shocked. Under the UN partition plan, their hometown of al-Ramla, along with neighboring Lydda (Lod) and the coastal city of Jaffa, would be part of the Arab Palestinian state.

The plan provided that 54.5 percent of Palestine and more than 80 percent of its cultivated citrus and grain plantations would go to the Jewish state. Jews represented about one-third of the population and owned 7 percent of the land. Most Arabs would not accept the partition.

If the plan went forward, al-Ramla would lie only a few miles from the new Jewish state. At least, Bashir's parents thought, it could have been worse; under the UN plan, the family would not be strangers on its own land. Still, what would happen to the Arabs in what was soon to be Jewish territory? The partition would place more than four hundred thousand Arabs in the new Jewish state, making them a 45 percent minority amid half a million Jews.

Reaction to the UN vote was swift. Palestinians, backed by other Arab leaders, immediately rejected the partition and pledged to fight it. Why, they asked, should their homeland be the solution to the Jewish problem in Europe?

Jews in Palestine and around the world welcomed the partition. In Bulgaria, Moshe and Solia were elated. At last, after the Holocaust, the world had seen the justice in the Zionist cause.

Zionist leaders had accepted the concept of a partition the year before, abandoning an earlier position that favored a "Jewish commonwealth" across all of Palestine. And Transjordan's King Abdullah secretly agreed to divide Palestine between a Jewish state and an expansion of Abdullah's desert kingdom.

David Ben-Gurion worried about the large Arab minority on the land set aside for Jews. "Such a composition does not provide a stable basis for a Jewish state," he said. "There can be no stable and strong Jewish state so long as it has a Jewish majority of only 60 [actually 55] percent."

Within hours of the UN announcement, Arabs attacked a Jewish bus near al-Ramla. Three days of protests by both sides led to violent clashes in Jerusalem, with fourteen people dead, Arabs and Jews. It was only the beginning.

Other Arab states and the former rebel leader made plans to mobilize troops in Palestine. Throngs of people filled the public squares of Arab capitals, shouting their approval. It appeared that Arab armies could eliminate the Jewish state before it was even established. Egypt's minister of war boasted that "the Egyptian military is capable on its own of occupying Tel Aviv, the capital of Jews, in fifteen days."

On the other side, Zionist forces had been preparing for months, mobilizing to secure arms and recruit young Jewish men, many of whom were Holocaust survivors fresh from displaced-persons camps. These battered-refugees-turned-soldiers were highly motivated to defend their new homeland. Ben-Gurion's Haganah developed battle plans, including the control of areas beyond the UN partition line, in a region designated as part of the Arab state.

The future of Palestine, it was increasingly clear, would be determined by facts on the ground, not by what the UN had put on paper. "The boundaries of the state," Ben-Gurion wrote, "will not be determined by a U.N. resolution, but by the force of arms."

Chapter 6
EXPULSION

One night in the spring of 1948, the Khairi home was jolted by a series of blasts coming from the edge of town. Soon the news arrived: The headquarters of a former rebel commander had been destroyed. Recruits from the Haganah had blown a rocket through the fence surrounding the headquarters and then had thrown explosives into the building, bringing it down in a series of devastating blasts. At least seventeen men were killed.

The Khairis and other residents of al-Ramla grew increasingly worried. A series of recent bombings had killed scores of Arabs and Jews in Jerusalem and other regions, and now the violence had hit close to home. If the rebels could not even guard their own headquarters, how could they protect the city?

Word soon came of other blows. The most revered commander of the Arabs was killed in the battle for Qastal. Control of the hill at Qastal meant control of the road, and therefore the supply lines between Jerusalem and the Mediterranean ports forty miles to the west. Even worse, a Jewish militia had massacred hundreds of women, children, and unarmed men in the village of Deir Yassin, near Jerusalem.

In one day, the Arabs of Palestine had lost their greatest commander, their most important battle, and dozens of innocent lives. And now al-Ramla seemed even more vulnerable. Ahmad and Zakia saw that the lives of their nine children might be in danger.

Scores of other families began drifting into al-Ramla. They had fled Na'ani, a village of orange groves and watermelon fields a few miles away, after a Jewish farmer galloped into the village on horseback, shouting, "The Jewish army is coming! You need to leave, or you will all be killed." The people of Na'ani knew the man as Khawaja Shlomo—Shlomo the Stranger. He lived in a neighboring kibbutz. The villagers were well aware of the recent massacre in Deir Yassin, so they fled for al-Ramla, carrying virtually nothing with them.

Now Ahmad Khairi scarcely recognized his town. Refugees slept under trees in the Khairi orchards, crowded the coffee shops and markets, and choked the streets near Ahmad's furniture shop.

Ahmad began to consider sending Zakia and the children to a temporary safe haven. Within forty-eight hours, the British would be leaving Palestine for good, and whatever little order their presence provided in al-Ramla would be gone.

On May 14, in the nearby coastal city of Tel Aviv, Ben-Gurion declared Israel's independence. "It is," he proclaimed, "the self-evident right of the Jewish people to be a nation, as all other nations, in its own Sovereign State." U.S. president Truman wrote to Zionist leader Chaim Weizmann, who would become the president of Israel: "I sincerely hope that the Palestine situation will work out on an equitable and peaceful basis."

Almost immediately, Arab nations attacked. Egyptian ground forces struck Israeli settlements and advanced toward Tel Aviv and Jerusalem, while Syrian and Iraqi forces entered Palestine from the east. Soldiers from King Abdullah's Arab Legion crossed the Jordan River and took up positions in Ramallah and other lands that Abdullah wanted for the "West Bank" of his desert kingdom.

On the same day, a Jewish militia approached al-Ramla.

Al-Ramla men lay behind sandbags in shallow trenches they had dug with oxen and hand tools. The volunteer fighters would soon undergo a serious test.

Bursts of machine-gun fire echoed near the train tracks close to the Khairi home. Then came earsplitting explosions as shells landed nearby. Two hundred Jewish fighters were trying to penetrate al-Ramla from the west, while others fought for control of the Jaffa-to-Jerusalem road to ensure the flow of goods and to stop Arab attacks on Jewish convoys. The fighting was fierce. "The whole city," one Israeli account declared, became "one big battlefield." It wasn't clear who was winning or how long al-Ramla's defenders could hold out.

The fight continued for four days. Zakia and the children left their house and moved in with relatives in the Khairi family compound. "There were a lot of explosions and shooting," Bashir remembered years later. "I couldn't tell where they were coming from. I was afraid. I was trying to understand. You're not in your house, your room, your bed. There was no freedom of movement. I remember so many bodies, too many to collect."

Sheikh Mustafa urged the people of al-Ramla not to abandon the city. By May 19, the Arab fighters had pushed back the Jewish militia and prevailed.

Still, Ahmad had seen enough. It was too dangerous to let Zakia and their children stay in the city. He hired two cars to take the family east, through the hills of Palestine to Ramallah. The trip itself would be dangerous, Ahmad knew; though Ramallah was only twenty miles away, the roads were bad and pockets of fighting were erupting in unpredictable places. But staying would be more risky than leaving.

A truce went into effect in June. All equipment was to remain in place, with a strict UN arms embargo in effect. But the Israelis secretly broke the embargo with shipments of rifles, machine guns, armored cars, artillery, tanks, planes, and millions of rounds of ammunition from the country then known as Czechoslovakia. The British pressured King Abdullah to comply with the embargo; the Arab Legion would therefore face any resumption of fighting with severe shortages of weapons and ammunition. But Abdullah had taken control of much of the West Bank, so he was content with the present situation. UN mediator Count Folke Bernadotte agreed, proposing the partition of Palestine between Israel and Transjordan. But that plan would leave the people of al-Ramla and Lydda as subjects of Abdullah and Transjordan, and not citizens of an independent Arab state as previously expected.

Israel rejected Bernadotte's proposal, and the Arab states voted to resume fighting for an Arab-majority state. Abdullah reluctantly agreed, and the war resumed. Lydda soon fell to Jewish battalions, and al-Ramla again came under attack. Arab Legion troops pulled out, and reinforcements never arrived.

At the Khairi compound, the remaining family members shuttered the windows and closed all the doors. Firdaws, a second cousin of the Khairis, heard Israeli soldiers shouting through bullhorns outside: *"Yallah Abdullah! Go to King Abdullah, go to Ramallah!"*

Soldiers were going house to house, in some cases pounding on doors with the butts of their guns, yelling at people to leave. Firdaws could hear them announcing the arrival of buses to take residents of al-Ramla to the front lines of the Arab Legion. No matter what the terms of surrender or what Sheikh Mustafa said, it looked as if they wouldn't have any choice. Their world was coming apart, but perhaps they could hold out a bit longer. Eventually, Sheikh Mustafa sent his son Husam to surrender.

Jewish soldiers went house to house, yelling at al-Ramla's residents to leave. They were being forced from their homes.

The morning of July 14 was cloudless and extremely hot. Thousands of people had been expelled from al-Ramla by bus and truck. Some, like Bashir and his siblings, had left well before the Jewish soldiers arrived, taking refuge in Ramallah. Others in the Khairi clan had remained in al-Ramla. Now they waited in the city's bus terminal. There were about thirty-five of them, including Sheikh Mustafa. They carried a few suitcases, bundles of clothes, and gold strapped to their bodies. They planned for a short trip, in miles and days, and were certain they would be returning soon, after the Arab armies recaptured al-Ramla.

The residents of al-Ramla had left behind their couches and tables; rugs; libraries; framed family pictures; and their blankets, dishes, and cups. They left their fezzes and galabias, balloon pants, spare keffiyehs, sashes, and belts. They left their spices for makloubeh, grape leaves in brine, and the flour for the dough of their date pastries. They left their fields of wild peas and jasmine, passiflora and dried scarlet anemone, mountain lilies that grew between the barley and the wheat.

They left their silk and linen, silver bracelets and chokers, amber, coral, and necklaces with Austrian coins. They left their pottery and soaps, leather and oils, Swedish ovens and copper pots, and drinking goblets from Bohemia. They left their silver trays filled with sugared almonds and sweet dried chickpeas; their dolls, made with glued-together wood chips; their sumac; their indigo.

The bus took them out of al-Ramla toward the front lines of the Arab Legion at Latrun. There, they were ordered off the bus and told to march north, toward Salbit, where trucks would take them to Ramallah. They were told the walk was only four miles, but by now it was one hundred degrees. There was no shade and no road, just a steep rise across cacti and Christ's thorn. This is what the people would later call "the donkey road"—if the donkey can make it, perhaps people can, too.

A line of humanity moved slowly up the hills in the waves of heat. The refugees bent forward under the sun, stumbling over rocks, thorns, and sharp wheat stalks cut short from the recent harvest.

White crusts formed around everyone's mouths. A woman gave birth on the ground. How far was Salbit? Were they still going in the right direction? They crossed fields of corn, where they plucked ripe ears and sucked the moisture out of the kernels.

The Khairis and others began to shed their belongings. After a time, someone found a well, but the rope on the pail was broken. Women removed their dresses, lowered them into the stagnant water, and lifted them back up, placing the fabric to their children's lips so they could suck on the wet cloth.

After staggering through the hills until evening, the Khairis came to a grove of fig trees in the village of Salbit. The village was nearly abandoned except for the hundreds of refugee families resting in the orchards. That night, the Khairi family sat under the fig trees, quietly smoking their water pipe.

The next morning, trucks from the Arab Legion took the people to Ramallah. They reached the crest of a hill just west of the city. Ramallah had long been a Christian hill town and a cool summer haven for Arabs. Now tens of thousands of refugees milled about, stunned and humiliated, looking for food and determined to return home.

Chapter 7
EMIGRATION

Sunlight filtered through the narrow windowpanes of Sofia's central rail station, casting a hazy glow on the hundreds of Jewish passengers packed inside the waiting hall. Moshe and Solia Eshkenazi inched forward in two long lines of Bulgarian Jews in the train station. It was October 1948.

Solia wore a long skirt and a matching tailored jacket, and her dark hair spilled over her shoulders from beneath a wide-brimmed hat. The passengers stood surrounded by boxes and suitcases. Moshe held the family's identity papers. He was short and square, with the dark olive skin, high cheekbones, and deep-set eyes of many Sephardic Jews. Beside them lay their infant, Dalia, asleep in her straw basket.

At long tables at the front of the lines sat uniformed Bulgarian immigration police. One by one, the Jews prepared to show their papers and open their suitcases for inspection for hidden cash or gold. They were not allowed to take anything of value, although some travelers had sewn jewels inside their underwear or strapped coins to their bodies.

No one was planning to return. When they reached the immigration tables, they would sign documents saying that from this day forward they would no longer be citizens of the People's Republic of Bulgaria. Later that day, they would board two long trains and ride to the coast of Yugoslavia, where a ship, the *Pan York*, would be waiting to take them to the new state of Israel.

Moshe and Solia were part of a history unlike any other in Europe. They knew that—like nearly everyone else in the railway station— they were lucky just to be alive. Solia believed that were it not for the decency of so many Gentiles in Bulgaria—and particularly of a handful of people who chose to act against the deportation in 1943—she and Moshe could have been on a train to a death camp, not waiting to board a ship with their infant daughter for a new life in Israel.

After Ben-Gurion declared Israel's independence and the war between the Arabs and the Jews officially began, the Jewish Agency and the Bulgarian government drew up detailed plans for an orderly emigration. First there were five small ships carrying 150 people each.

Some recall it as a chain reaction, others as a deliberate, joyous step toward freedom, others as a fever. For years, the decision to emigrate had been theoretical. Even after it became possible, many Jews said they planned to stay in Bulgaria. But that changed quickly. A neighbor decided to take his family on an early ship. Then the housewife across the street announced that her family was going. A cousin departed, then the local electrician. Then the tailor was gone. The shoemaker. A police officer. Now the rabbi. The fruit peddler. The Bulgarian Jewish choir—all one hundred members—away, together, on a boat to Israel.

By the spring of 1948, there was little left for Moshe and Solia to debate. Hard times showed few signs of lifting. Factories had been nationalized and property seized for the state. Moshe's future liveli-hood was uncertain, and he viewed the new government as excessively brutal. He wanted someplace new. He'd spent most of his life hear-ing about a new life in a distant place. Moshe thrived on challenges, and he trusted his instincts, which in this case told him to go.

Solia was less sure. Leaving behind her beloved country weighed heavily on her. But she would follow Moshe's lead. As soon as they could, the family would move to Israel.

The first major operation, the Bulgarian government decided, would be arranged through the port of Yugoslavia. A total of 3,694 Bulgarian Jews would have about three weeks to get their affairs in order. Before leaving, they would be required to submit to medical examinations to certify that they were free of tuberculosis, heart disease, typhoid, and other diseases. Then they would close their homes, say goodbye, and assemble on October 25, 1948, at the cen-tral railway station in Sofia, where trains would be waiting.

Now Moshe and Solia moved forward in the crush of passengers on the station's platform. They said goodbye to Moshe's brother and his wife, who had come to see them off. The atmosphere was heavy with sorrow but buoyant with expectation: brothers and fathers and grandmothers and uncles knew they could be embracing for the last time.

The air was sharp and bright. South of the platform, the crest of Vitosha Mountain rose up, its jagged crown off-center like the peak of a rumpled hat.

The train left Sofia in the afternoon, moving slowly at first, then picking up speed as it puffed and clacked west, whistling out of the capital city toward the border of Yugoslavia and a boat bound for Israel.

For many of the 1,800 Bulgarian Jews on that train with Moshe, Solia, and Dalia—or the tens of thousands of Hungarian, Romanian, or Polish Jews migrating in the fall of 1948—the journey to Israel represented a return after two thousand years of exile, a chance to fulfill the Talmudic promise: "He who makes four steps in Israel, all of his sins will be forgiven."

The train reached the bluffs of the Dalmatian coast at dusk. To the west, at the horizon of the Adriatic Sea, the sky was ablaze with color. Behind Solia and Moshe in the darkened east lay Bulgaria. Somewhere back there the family's precious belongings, about 440 pounds of them, lay in crates, waiting to be shipped. Solia had packed a hope chest made of straw with wool blankets and a woven Bulgarian rug. She had also packed special wedding china from Czechoslovakia, the color of cream, with tiny red flowers along the rims; a soup tureen and bowls; etched purple crystal, for sipping Bulgarian brandy; pillow covers, doilies, and other knitted handwork; and a pink bedroom set: two wardrobes, bedboard, and frame.

Solia and Moshe weren't the only ones separated from their belongings. Four thousand tons of crates would soon be stacked up in the Sofia synagogue where they'd been married. Workers scrambled to find freighters to haul the crates to Israel.

The train hissed to a stop near the port. Through the windows, perhaps three hundred yards away, Moshe and Solia could see a great masted ship floating at the pier, its lights shining against the night sky.

The *Pan York* was as long as a football field, its three masts towering over the deck. Below, its cargo holds, with a capacity of 11 million pounds, had been converted to carry 3,694 Bulgarian Jews.

Solia and Moshe followed the line of emigrants up the gangplank.

As they stepped onto the ship, they were hit by the strong odor of disinfectant. Before them loomed a huge metal cargo hold painted sea green. Wooden bunk beds were stacked three high for as far as they could see. This would be their home for the next eight days.

In the ship's storehouses, the crew had stacked thousands of cans of supplies, paid for by the American Jewish Joint Distribution Committee, or JDC. For the next week, Moshe, Solia, and the rest of the passengers would survive on tinned meat and fish, canned milk, juice, bread, margarine, grapefruit marmalade, and small pieces of dark chocolate. The JDC also supplied soap and emergency medical supplies.

Dalia slept through most of the journey. Her parents said she was the only one on the ship who didn't get seasick.

Slowly the Yugoslav coast disappeared from view. The *Pan York* cut south through the Adriatic. From the bow there was only the sky, the horizon, and the late-October seas.

Moshe had no idea where his family would live, or what awaited them upon their arrival in Haifa. He knew that the war was still going on, though Israel had the advantage and new truce talks suggested a settlement soon. It seemed obvious to Moshe that some kind of Jewish state would survive.

Despite the conflict, many Jewish intellectuals in Palestine had argued that Israel's long-term survival depended on finding a way to coexist with the Arabs. Moshe was part of a Zionist organization that had advocated a binational democratic state for all the people of Palestine. But after the Soviets voted to partition the region into two separate states, Moshe had thought: *This is the beginning of a long war.*

Before dawn on the eighth day of the journey, lights appeared in the distance. The passengers began to stir and climb up on deck. As land grew closer, they could see that some of the lights appeared to be sitting on top of others. The scattered jewels in the air were actually lights from houses on different elevations of the hillside. They were almost there.

As daylight broke on November 4, passengers crowded toward the bow as the boat powered into Haifa's port. Some were crying. Others began to sing "Hatikva," for sixty years the anthem of the Zionists and now of the new state of Israel.

It felt to many that after all their struggles they had finally come home.

Onshore, officials of the Jewish Agency sat at tables behind a roped line, processing the passengers family by family. They took names and years of birth; Dalia's birth year was recorded, incorrectly, as 1948. The Eshkenazis received an identity card and were told to proceed to the large metal building just ahead. There, workers with pump sprayers doused the Bulgarians with a substance that turned everyone's hair stiff and white. Children ran around, laughing and pointing to one another's DDT hairstyles.

Next they were given sandwiches. Some families were put on buses, others on a yellow narrow-gauge train that chugged south along the coast. The Eshkenazis rode toward an old British military barracks about thirty miles away, where they spent the next ten days in a tent alongside a thousand others in the gathering of nations—dark, curly-haired, Arabic-speaking immigrants from Morocco; pale, dazed Yiddish speakers from Romania, Hungary, and Poland. It was a crowded, smelly place, hot for early November and muddy from the rains.

Soon Moshe and Solia grew restless. They were anxious to settle somewhere. Tel Aviv had little space, and Jerusalem was still too dangerous. After ten days, Moshe noticed people sitting at a table, signing up immigrants to move to a town somewhere between this immigrant camp and Jerusalem.

Moshe had never heard of the town. *But why not?* he thought. *Let us try this place called Ramla.*

Chapter 8
REFUGE

Members of the Khairi family stepped down from the flatbed truck near the center of Ramallah and stood in the glare of the scorching heat. They could scarcely believe the scene in front of them. Entire families were camped on the ground, huddling around large metal dinner plates to spoon a few fava beans and lentils into their mouths with scraps of bread. Refugees were sitting and lying beneath trees, in doorways, and beside the road. Families had been split up, and now they didn't know where to find each other.

Sheikh Mustafa walked through the city center toward the Grand Hotel, where he managed to find a small room. Then he set out to find his nephew and family. Ahmad and Zakia had arrived earlier with Bashir and their other children and had rented a room near the Quaker School. Over the last two months, Ahmad had been going back and forth to al-Ramla, bringing food, a few clothes, and other household items back to Ramallah.

One hundred thousand refugees crowded Ramallah's schoolyards, gymnasiums, convents, army barracks, and any other space they could find. Some fortunate ones shared quarters with relatives; family homes now packed ten or fifteen people into each room. But most of the newly homeless slept in the open air, in olive groves, barnyards, and on the bare ground. They were dependent on springs for water, waiting in long lines for turns to fill cans. Officials feared that the water would run out, and that there wasn't enough food to keep anyone alive for long. The scant water supply, according to UN investigators, stood "unprotected and unorganized, infected and a menace to health . . . an epidemic of typhoid is almost inevitable."

Sheikh Mustafa found Ahmad, Zakia, and the children sharing a single room. At home in al-Ramla, Bashir had had his own room and bed; now he slept with the others on a pair of mattresses. Other Khairis slept in adjacent rooms. Under the circumstances, this represented relative comfort, made possible by family connections and wealth.

Bashir watched his mother stave off the family's hunger by selling her jewelry in exchange for bread, olives, cooking oil, and vegetables. Bashir understood that Zakia had become the family bank and its main source of provisions. She wasn't alone. Each day Bashir saw women returning from the springs with jugs of water balanced on their heads, or hawking handmade sweets at a makeshift street market.

A few people found work with local villagers during the olive harvest. Others went begging from house to house when there was no alternative. "We have lost our homes," they said. "Can you help us out with some oil, lentils, flour, fava?"

Sometimes the beggars suffered the abuse of an increasingly angry local population, who themselves were overwhelmed by the unfolding calamity. "You sold your land to the Jews and came here!" they would taunt. "Why couldn't you defend yourselves?"

The dispossessed men, in particular, had been shocked into silence, their defeat and humiliation at the hands of the Jews compounded by the disdain of the locals. Bashir would remember the peasant men with glazed eyes, sitting on burlap sacks in the shade of olive trees. At home, it was harvest time for sesame, melons, grapes, cactus fruit, and summer vegetables. This was the men's lifework and what they knew how to do. In sudden exile in Ramallah, they were idle and their families hungry. Their wives endured endless waits at food distribution centers as trucks rumbled up the narrow road from Amman, fifty miles to the east, to deliver large flat biscuits, unleavened loaves, and the occasional sack of tomatoes or eggplants, courtesy of the Red Cross and King Abdullah of Transjordan.

The rations were meant to stave off starvation, but the refugees were mostly left to live off their wits. They begged and stole from the locals, stripped the fruit trees bare, and, in some cases, scoured the trash bins of Abdullah's Arab Legion troops for scraps of food.

The Khairis were not enduring that level of hunger, but Bashir began to understand the humiliation of the refugee. For a six-year-old boy, a seemingly simple deprivation would take on enormous meaning. One day his father told Zakia in frustration that he didn't have enough money to buy his friends a cup of coffee. For a Palestinian man, Bashir knew, inviting friends for coffee was an elementary gesture of hospitality, and the inability to do so represented a profound humiliation. Bashir would remember this shame for the rest of his life.

Many of the refugees felt betrayed by King Abdullah, who had promised to protect them. And they still expected to return to al-Ramla. Eventually Abdullah reached out to Sheikh Mustafa with a personal offer. "Cousin," the king said, evoking their distant relations that went back centuries, "I cannot allow you to be miserable refugees. Bring your whole family and I will give you a palace in Amman to stay in."

Mustafa, the longtime mayor of al-Ramla, was not inclined to ignore the thousands of other refugees. "I am not alone with my family," he reminded the king. "I have all the people of al-Ramla to take care of. Shall I bring them, too?"

"Stay where you are," came the king's reply.

Nonetheless, the Khairis and thousands of other refugees assumed they would be returning home soon—either due to a victory by the Arab armies or as a result of a political agreement.

"Return," Bashir said, "was the issue, from day one."

Strong signs, however, pointed to Israel's determination not to surrender al-Ramla, Lydda, or dozens of other villages in Arab Palestine. A confidential U.S. State Department message cited "Jewish measures designed to prevent [refugees'] return . . . much of their property [is] under the control of the Israeli Government which . . . would not relinquish it willingly to the Arabs."

David Ben-Gurion said, "I will be in favor of them not returning even after the war," and his foreign minister flatly stated, "This is our policy: They are not coming back."

Israeli officials soon would not even acknowledge that the forced expulsions had taken place, reporting to the International Red Cross "that approximately 300,000 Arabs left their places of residence in the territory occupied by Israeli forces, *but not one of them has been deported or requested to leave his place of residence.* [The emphasis is from the original document.] On the contrary, in most of the places the Arab inhabitants were given to understand that there is no reason whatsoever for their flight."

At summer's end in al-Ramla, several hundred Arabs were still locked behind a barbed-wire fence. Most of the families were Christian; they were considered less of a threat to the new Israeli state than the Muslims of al-Ramla. The fenced-in area was now called the *sakne*, or "Arab ghetto." It was near the Khairis' street, down which Ahmad had walked to his furniture workshop.

Ahmad's house stood in silence, part of an empty neighborhood. Doors were agape and belongings scattered about after looters had their pick. Shop merchandise lay rotting in the street. Military trucks rolled back and forth, laden with beds, mattresses, cupboards, couches, and drapes.

In the late summer and early fall of 1948, Palestinian men tried to return from exile. Many crossed porous front lines—Bashir believes that his father was one of them—entering their villages and fields at night to gather belongings or harvest what they could. The Israeli government considered them "infiltrators," and some were shot on sight. Others returned to find their crops burned.

If hungry villagers were allowed to return to their conquered fields, warned an Israeli report, the next step could be "resettlement in the villages, something which could seriously endanger many of our achievements during the first six months of the war." Instead, the chief of staff for the Israeli Defense Forces called upon Jews to work those fields, declaring, "Every enemy field in the area of our complete control we must harvest. . . . In any event, the Arabs must be prevented from reaping those fields."

A few Israelis raised their voices in alarm. "We still do not properly appreciate what kind of enemy we are now nurturing outside the borders of our state," the agriculture minister, Aharon Cizling, warned in a cabinet meeting. "Our enemies, the Arab states, are a mere nothing compared with those hundreds of thousands of Arabs [that is, Palestinian refugees] who will be moved by hatred and hopelessness and infinite hostility to wage war on us, regardless of any agreement that might be reached."

By mid-September Bashir began to hear his parents talk about moving out of Ramallah to a place where they could live more comfortably until they were able to return to al-Ramla. They were still living in a single room.

UN mediator Count Bernadotte reported that several countries had sent emergency supplies for the Palestinians: Australia provided one thousand tons of wheat; France, one hundred fifty tons of fruit; Italy, twenty tons of olive oil; Ireland, two hundred tons of potatoes; the Netherlands, fifty tons each of peas and beans; Indonesia, six hundred tons of rice and sugar; Norway, fifty tons of fish; South Africa, fifty tons of meat. The United States and the American Red Cross provided additional food and medical supplies.

Bernadotte continued to advance a division of historic Palestine between Israel and Transjordan. Under this plan, the Khairis and other refugees would go back to al-Ramla and Lydda, but not to an independent state, as many Palestinian Arabs had fought for, but to an Arab state under the rule of Abdullah and his kingdom of Transjordan. (Later, after the war, "Trans" was dropped from the name and the kingdom became known as Jordan.)

Bernadotte's proposals were based on what he saw as the realities of the day. "A Jewish state called Israel exists in Palestine," he wrote, "and there are no sound reasons for assuming that it will not continue to do so." He stressed an additional point that would have been of great interest to Ahmad, Zakia, and the thousands of refugees sleeping on the ground in Ramallah: "The right of innocent people, uprooted by the present terror and ravage of war, to return to their homes, should be affirmed and made effective, with assurance of adequate compensation for the property of those who may choose not to return."

⁓☙

The day after Bernadotte made that statement, he was assassinated in Jerusalem. The Jewish militia group known as the Stern Gang claimed responsibility and called UN observers "members of foreign occupation forces." In response, Ben-Gurion detained two hundred members of the Stern Gang, including one of its leaders, future prime minister Yitzhak Shamir, and ordered the other extremist Jewish militia, Irgun (led by another future prime minister, Menachem Begin), to disband and turn over its weapons to the Israeli army.

After Bernadotte's assassination, international pressure mounted on Israel to accept his last proposal. This would have required Israel to give back conquered territory that included al-Ramla and Lydda. But battles soon resumed, and Bernadotte's proposal, like countless other "peace plans" that would follow, dissolved into history.

Meantime, in the midst of all this violence and political maneuvering, more and more Jews from across the global diaspora continued to pour into the new nation.

Chapter 9
ARRIVAL

The busload of Jewish immigrants approached the town of Ramla from roads to the north and west. It slowed as it reached a military blockade at the edge of town. Inside the bus were the first Israeli civilians to come to the conquered city—including Moshe and Solia Eshkenazi and their infant daughter, Dalia.

As the bus rolled past the checkpoint, Moshe and Solia looked out at a ghost town. Sheep, dogs, chickens, and cats roamed the streets. Soldiers watched over rows of empty dwellings. Stone houses stood open, their contents spilling out into the yards.

The bus passed cactus hedges and lines of olive and orange trees, then it stopped and everyone got out. A representative of the Jewish Agency told them they were free to enter any house, inspect it, and claim it. The paperwork would come later.

Moshe and Solia came upon a house to their liking. It was in good shape and virtually empty, though not brand-new. Clearly, someone had lived there before. It was a stone house with an open layout and plenty of space. In the backyard there was a lemon tree.

Lying in bed in their new home, the couple knew they hadn't

arrived at the safe haven they had sought. Israeli and Egyptian forces were fighting just south of Ramla, and the line of defense was perilously close to their new home.

After two weeks in Ramla, Moshe and Solia celebrated Dalia's first birthday. It was December 2, 1948, a year and three days after the UN partition vote and the beginning of the battles over the shape of historic Palestine.

The family had received a steel-framed bed; blankets; a kerosene lamp; a camping stove; four large candles; and a ration card for sugar, oil, powdered eggs, and milk. Another family of three had moved into an adjacent room in the same house. Solia's mother, brother, two sisters, and a brother-in-law were making final plans to leave Bulgaria, and the house would soon shelter eleven people.

Eventually the families would sign agreements with the state, which had declared itself the "custodian" of the houses it considered "abandoned property." The Eshkenazis lived on "K.B. Street." This was a temporary name; a committee would soon prepare lists of Jewish historical figures and recently fallen war heroes to replace the Arabic names on the street signs.

The town was under military rule in an emerging nation still at war. The spoils of conquest, and of sudden flight, were still being hauled away. Soldiers piled couches, dressers, and other heavy items into the backs of army trucks.

Some of the new arrivals found temporary work sweeping out the Arab houses to prepare for more busloads of immigrants; their children sold cigarettes brought on the boats to soldiers standing guard. To the children, it was all an adventure. They roamed the streets feeling like discoverers, taking over an abandoned house to set up a secret club, searching the rooms for marbles or other treasures left behind. Often when they returned, they would find the house occupied by immigrants. These new arrivals, many of whom were survivors of the concentration camps in Europe, asked few questions. Most found empty houses to live in, then went looking for work.

In the early months, jobs were scarce and seasonal. A few people were employed building and paving roads. Others hitchhiked or rode bicycles to the Jewish citrus groves to pick fruit. Children would recall fathers and uncles with one hand on the handlebar and the other balancing a ladder, pedaling toward the orchards. Some were accustomed to that kind of work, but others, working a strange land in dark European shoes and fraying suit coats, were overwhelmed. As a result, Jewish farmers, who had depended on cheap Arab labor, struggled to make their harvest.

Moshe Eshkenazi first worked for the Jewish Agency, delivering iron bed frames to immigrant families. Soon the job expanded to full-time work for the Custodian of Abandoned Properties. He helped respond to the needs of new arrivals, who, like his own family, had moved into the houses of the Arabs. Moshe helped repair the houses where necessary, arranging to fix leaks and shore up walls. As for the former residents, the Israeli government designated them as "absentees." They had simply run away, Moshe and Solia were told.

Local Israeli officials began to worry about the consequences of their policy toward the Arabs of Israel. "They still have not gotten used to reality and have become apathetic about the future," wrote an official named S. Zamir in a status report on the Arab community of Ramla. "The government's declaration of equality and freedom is like a voice calling out in the desert unless we prove it by actions. Their economic situation is very bad. They have enough provisions for the time being, but soon the question will arise: 'What will we eat?'"

After their release from the POW camp, the Arab men of Ramla, like Arabs across Israel at the time, were nevertheless still confined with their families to a few fenced-in blocks. These included Bashir's uncle Rasem, a doctor who had stayed after the expulsions. For several years, the Arabs of Israel would live under martial law. Arab residents wishing to leave their neighborhood or villages were required to apply to the military authorities for special permits. Movement was restricted on security grounds. Some leaders in the new state continued to argue for the "transfer" of the remaining Arabs across the Jordan River to Abdullah's kingdom.

The Arabs of the Ramla and Lod "ghettos" found their former homes occupied by Jewish families and their agricultural lands controlled by kibbutzim. Not at home, not in exile, they were defined by the Israeli government as "present absentees." Many sought legal recourse to move back into their houses or resume farming their lands.

"Though on several occasions since his interview with the Military Governor, Mr. Shomski promised me to return the door and shutters and to re-condition my house," wrote an Arab resident of Lydda in December 1949, "up to this date nothing has been done. On the contrary, owing to the absence of doors and windows unknown persons have carried out extensive damage to my house. . . . I shall be very much obliged if you will give your instructions . . . to return my doors and window shutters as soon as possible."

"I beg to submit the following for your kind consideration," wrote an al-Ramla landowner, an Arab whose plea had begun in March 1949. "I am the registered owner of the following pieces of land: Parcel

No. 69; Block No. 4374; Locality Ramle; Area 5,032 Sq. Metres. . . .
All these parcels, including my own share, were treated by the Apet-
ropos [Custodian of Abandoned Properties] as Absentee Properties
in spite of the fact that I am not an absentee. . . ."

"I am the registered owner of Half of Parcel 13," wrote an Arab
appellant to the local council of Kibbutz Gezer, five miles southeast
of Ramla. "I am prepared to pay the Local Council's taxes on my share
in the Parcel. . . . I shall be obliged also to know who has ploughed
my land and with whose authority he did so."

The Eshkenazis and others living in the Arab homes did not give
the past owners much thought. Instead, they focused on building a
new society. Job prospects began to improve slightly, especially for
the first to arrive, as they found ways to use the skills they brought
with them from Europe as mechanics, electricians, plumbers, and
shopkeepers. By the summer of 1949, 697 of the 2,093 families registered with the city had found work in Ramla. There were 25 Jewish
shoemakers; 15 carpenters; 10 seamstresses; and several bakers,
butchers, watchmakers, and sausage makers. Seventeen cafés had
opened along with 36 groceries, a pharmacy, and a law office.

Solia opened a shop for baby clothes in the old Arab *sakne*, or
ghetto, before taking a job with the new national tax authority. Dalia's
aunt Stella went to work mopping floors at the hospital before opening a makeshift beauty salon in her bedroom. Dalia would watch as
Bulgarian women came to the house for haircuts and conversation.
Soon Stella's sister Dora opened her own beauty shop in an old Arab
storefront, and Stella joined her there. The customers would often sit
for hours, and if someone had just arrived from Bulgaria, the news
would be accompanied by bitter jokes about the communist regime.

In the first session of the new Israeli parliament (known by its

Hebrew name, Knesset), legislators authorized dozens of ministries, including Agriculture, Defense, Immigration, Justice, Religions, Social Welfare, and War Victims. It passed laws authorizing an army and mandatory service in that army; systems for taxation, customs, compulsory education, and the courts; an independence day; and, perhaps most famously, the Law of Return, whereby citizenship "shall be granted to every Jew who expressed his desire to settle in Israel." The law would become an endless source of bitterness between Israel and the Arab world for the next half century and beyond. For the Palestinian Arabs in exile, the law, and each wave of Jews admitted to the new state, denied their own dreams of return. For the Israelis, the law ensured a core aspect of their identity by providing a safe haven for every Jew who wished to make *aliyah*, the Jewish migration to Israel.

By the end of 1949, as Dalia turned two and her "pioneer" parents marked their first year in Ramla, new arrivals had boosted the city's population past ten thousand. In a photograph from around that time, Dalia's father stands beside her, his dark wavy hair combed back, his cuffed pants hoisted above his waist, his smile frozen in time. In the background, behind the lemon tree, Moshe had planted bananas and guava fruit. To the right, at the edge of the frame, stood a henhouse where the Eshkenazis raised their own chickens. It was the time of the *tsena*, or scarcity, and everyone was expected to pitch in.

During the *tsena*, the Ministry of Supply and Rationing moved to the center of Israeli life. The ministry's job was to regulate the limited supply of food so no one went hungry. Israel's rapid growth required it to import 85 percent of its food. The state had reduced its trade with the markets of the British Empire, and Arab countries had imposed economic and political boycotts. Egypt was blockading cargo to Israel through the Suez Canal, despite a UN resolution calling for free passage through the vital waterway. Israel depended on wheat and processed flour, and imported meats, seasonally discounted fish, and even olive oil, from the United States, Canada, and Australia. With the demise of the Arab groves, Israel could supply only 8 percent of its own olive oil demands.

The Eshkenazis, like many Israelis during the early 1950s, innovated their way through the scarcity. Solia bartered with a neighbor for milk and butter from the neighbor's cow, offering eggs from her own family's chickens in exchange.

In the Ramla market, Dalia would walk with her father, passing the stalls of cucumbers, olives, and watermelons; past the mounds of oranges and bananas and the hawkers yelling, "Sabra! Sabra!" before the fresh cactus fruit; and into the dry goods stores for fabric and shoes.

In the evenings, Moshe and Solia would invite Bulgarian friends to gatherings in the backyard. They laid out plates of black olives, watermelon, and Bulgarian cheese, pouring cold glasses of *boza*, a sweet Balkan drink made from wheat. Often during these gatherings Dalia would walk to the side of the house, half listening to the adults, and inhale from the "candles of the night," the flowers that opened only after sunset. Solia would put a record on the phonograph and sultry Spanish music—a legacy of the Eshkenazis' Sephardic roots—would drift out of the house.

By 1955, the year Dalia turned eight, Moshe was rising into the leadership of the local office of the Custodian of Abandoned Properties. Dalia would visit during school vacations, intent on helping her father by answering phones or showing clients to his office. Usually they were women, often frustrated by leaks that had needed fixing for months or who were still living in a tent though they'd been promised better housing. Moshe would explain that his budget was distressingly low, but he'd "promise to deal with this even if the world turns upside down."

Dalia was amazed to see clients leave the office calmed by the sincere, overwhelmed bureaucrat and hoping for the best. On the street people constantly approached Moshe, shaking his hand and thanking him for his help.

On other afternoons, Dalia would stop at the hair salon her aunts had opened. The salon catered mostly to Bulgarians, but the two sisters were gaining a reputation, and soon Polish, Romanian, and Moroccan women would come and the language would switch from Bulgarian to broken French and broken Hebrew.

Dalia had begun to notice that some of her neighbors were silent about the past, where her own family spoke openly about their rescue in Bulgaria. At school, she had a teacher who, it was whispered, had lost his wife and children in the death camps in Poland. He was Dalia's favorite, always looking forward. "He gave us a feeling that he believed in our future," Dalia remembered. "He was a strict disciplinarian, but very affirmative. He gave us tools for life."

Many of Dalia's classmates, however, seemed almost out of reach. The children of Poles, Romanians, and Hungarians, they had come to the country, like Dalia, in the first days of the Israeli state. In the eyes of these children, Dalia saw a vacancy.

Sometimes at night Dalia heard the father of a classmate who lived next door screaming ceaselessly at the boy. She found this trauma a direct challenge to her faith. Though her parents had never been religious, Dalia's own belief in God had, she felt, always been a part of her. Few people in Ramla seemed to want to talk about what had happened in Europe during the war, but Dalia had seen the people with numbers tattooed on their arms. As she grew older, she learned about the atrocities in Germany, Poland, Romania, and Hungary. She found this truth indigestible. *For God to allow this to happen,* she would recall thinking, *is utterly unconscionable.* She was furious. "You have created human beings," she would shout to God. "You have to take responsibility for Your creation! You have to be more active in preventing such things!"

In school, Dalia learned of the silence of European Christians during the Holocaust, especially that of Pope Pius XII, who did not show the courage of the Bulgarian Orthodox Church. When she enrolled in piano lessons at St. Joseph's Catholic monastery in Ramla, she felt a deep ambivalence about Christianity. Entering the monastery, however, she was drawn in by the silence; by the painted statue of St. Joseph on a pedestal; by the dimly lit corridors with their black and white tiles; and by the portrait of another pope, John XXIII, whose face contained something humane. She began to understand something fundamental. Decades later, she would remember this moment as the beginning of a life of *discernment*: of being able to see the whole and not judge someone or something based simply on one observation or teaching.

As she grew up, Dalia frequently asked her parents and teachers: "What are these houses we are living in?"

"These are Arab houses," she was told.

"What *are* these Arab houses that everyone talks about?" she would reply.

Dalia's school was also in an Arab house, and there she learned of Israel's history. She learned about the creation of the state as a safe haven for Jews. She studied the War of Independence as the story of the few against the many. The Arabs had invaded, Dalia would read, in order to destroy the new state and throw the Jews into the sea. Most nations confronted with such hostilities would have been paralyzed, but tiny Israel had withstood five Arab armies. Little David had defeated Goliath.

As for the Arabs, Dalia's textbooks reported that they had run away, deserting their lands and abandoning their homes. The Arabs, one textbook of the day declared, "preferred to leave" once the Jews had taken their towns.

Dalia accepted the history she was taught. But why, she wondered, would anyone leave so willingly?

One afternoon when she was about seven or eight years old, Dalia climbed up the metal gate that Ahmad Khairi had placed at the end of the stone path in the front yard. Atop the gate perched a delicate piece of wrought iron in the shape of a star and crescent: the symbol of Islam. It bothered Dalia. "This is not an Arab house," she said to herself. She grasped the crescent and began wrenching it back and forth until it came loose in her hands. She clambered down and threw the crescent away.

Yet the questions about who lived in her house before, and where that family was now, continued to haunt Dalia.

Chapter 10
GAZA

Near the end of 1948, Ahmad and Zakia, unable to find decent work and overwhelmed by the misery around them, decided to move the family to Gaza, a strip of land on the Mediterranean coast wedged between Israel and Egypt's Sinai Peninsula. It would be much warmer in Gaza, and Ahmad had better job prospects there. Relatives with property could help them find a modest home to live in rent-free.

The Khairi family arrived in Gaza in December and moved into a one-room house with bare walls, concrete floors, and a roof of corrugated tin. Ahmad and Zakia gathered a few mattresses, borrowed pots and pans and a camping stove, found an old icebox, and started looking for work.

In the span of a few months, two hundred thousand refugees had poured into this narrow band of sand dunes and orange groves, more than tripling its population. They scoured the landscape, collecting, according to a UN report, "every movable object that could be burnt" for fuel. Thousands of people camped in long rows of tents. All supplies had to travel three hundred miles through the Egyptian desert and cross Gaza's only border with the Arab world—the Sinai Peninsula, to the southwest.

Bashir and his family heard constant shelling as Israel and Egypt clashed near Gaza city. Though the Egyptians controlled the Gaza Strip, there were frequent incursions by both sides across battle lines. Egypt, led by King Farouk, was fighting for territory, and not just with Israel; Farouk was also worried about King Abdullah of Jordan and his own quest for territory.

Palestinian nationalists, meanwhile, still aspired to establish an independent, Arab-majority state across the whole of Palestine. Egypt had permitted a small Palestinian independence group to establish a government-in-exile in Gaza, mostly to help thwart Abdullah. Abdullah responded by declaring himself "King of United Palestine."

As Arab governments jockeyed and maneuvered, the refugees never stopped longing for home. The right of return originally advocated by Count Bernadotte was enshrined by the United Nations in December 1948. UN Resolution 194 declared that "refugees wishing to return to their homes and live at peace with their neighbors should be permitted to do so at the earliest practical date, and that compensation should be paid for the property of those choosing not to return." The resolution—known simply as "one-nine-four"—generated tremendous hope for the Khairis and refugees across Arab Palestine. It was already clear, however, that Israel had no intention of implementing Resolution 194 and that the United Nations had no power to enforce it.

Ahmad found a job in Gaza using his carpentry skills to make wicker furniture for other refugees. The United Nations Relief and Work Agency (UNRWA) paid him not in cash but in extra rations of flour, rice, sugar, and fat. Zakia continued to sell off her gold, but the proceeds went only for essential items. The extreme situation led to what would have previously been unthinkable: the family sought and received permission from Sheikh Mustafa for Zakia and her daughters to take jobs. Bashir couldn't recall a single day when his mother and sisters weren't working. They now made money embroidering table covers or knitting sweaters and scarves.

For the refugees—both those who were destitute in the camps and those who were more well-off, like the Khairis—the central trauma was not in selling off their gold or finding enough to eat. Rather, it lay in the longing for home and in the indignity of dispossession.

The disruption of normal family life was having profound effects on the children.

The Khairi siblings breathed in the atmosphere of humiliation and defeat. For Bashir, avenging the loss of Palestine became a singular goal, even in play. His siblings and other neighborhood children would find pieces of wood to fashion as guns so they could play "Arabs and Jews" in the dirt streets. Bashir insisted that he always play the Arab.

In the spring of 1949, Sheikh Mustafa died. Had the family still been living in al-Ramla, his body would have been washed, dressed in white cloth, carried to the mosque for prayers, then immediately taken to the cemetery and placed in the earth, all according to Muslim custom. Instead, the family arranged for the body to be transported in a closed wooden coffin to the family cemetery in al-Ramla, where the Israelis would allow him his final place of rest.

"He died of a heart attack," Bashir said. "But really, it was from a broken heart."

By summer, Jordan, Egypt, Syria, and Iraq had signed armistice agreements with Israel; the war was officially over. With its capture of territory beyond the UN partition line, Israel was now in control of 78 percent of Palestine. The next year, in April 1950, King Abdullah completed his annexation of the West Bank, infuriating Palestinian nationalists. A year later, one of those nationalists shot Abdullah to death. Assassinations of the leaders of Egypt and Syria soon followed. In Gaza, the Egyptians responded by repressing all forms of political expression, and Palestinian nationalism was forced underground.

Two governments were essentially in place in Gaza: the Egyptians, who imposed the equivalent of martial law on the stateless Palestinians; and the UNRWA, which was now responsible for feeding, training, and educating the hundreds of thousands of refugees.

"Their clothing . . . has become shabby and ragged," declared a UN report in 1951. "The majority of the men employed on Agency road-building projects had no shoes. Both blankets and the tent flies issued as additional protection are often diverted from their proper use and cut up for clothing. The most fortunate are the children in schools (less than half the total number of children on the rolls), who have generally been given both clothing and footwear."

In Gaza city, Bashir and two of his siblings shared the same one-room class in a UNRWA school. Teachers, mostly refugees themselves, doled out UNRWA pencils, clothing, fish oil, vitamins, and milk. Bashir recalled learning the history of the Nakba, or Catastrophe, which he, his classmates, and the Palestinian teachers could speak of from personal experience and with deep conviction: *The Jews expelled us. We have a right to return.*

"Palestine is our country," the refugee children recited each day.

"Our aim is to return. Death does not frighten us. Palestine is ours, we shall never forget her. Another homeland we will never accept! Our Palestine, witness, O God and History, we promise to shed our blood for you!"

Bashir was a good student, and his teachers considered him especially attentive.

He turned ten in 1952. By now the dream of immediate return had transformed into the reality of long-term struggle. The Palestinians had begun to understand that their return would not come about through diplomatic pressure. Though the "right of return" dominated most conversations in the street, markets, and coffeehouses, it was clear that no government in the world was prepared to force Israel to accept the terms of the UN resolution guaranteeing that return.

For the Israelis, the idea of return was moot. In a letter to the UN's Palestine Conciliation Commission, a top Israeli official wrote that "it would be doing the refugees a disservice to let them persist in the belief that if they returned, they would find their homes or shops or fields intact. . . . Generally, it can be said that any Arab house that survived the impact of the war . . . now shelters a Jewish family."

It was clearer than ever—Israel would never agree to allow Palestinian refugees the one thing they wanted most: to return to their homes and land.

Chapter 11
TENSION

In the spring of 1956, when Dalia was in third grade, she began to make a connection between the Arabs she had learned about in school and those her parents talked about at home. Israeli newspapers were full of stories about the raids of infiltrators from Gaza backed by the new Egyptian president, Gamal Abdel Nasser. Nasser had a plan for Arab unity that would include the "liberation of Palestine" and the return of the refugees.

Moshe read about the incursions onto Israeli soil by Egyptian and Palestinian guerrillas bent on wiping out the Jewish state, and about the swift Israeli responses. As the Suez Canal crisis made the news, he and Solia understood that there would be cause for their nation to go to war. Nasser was defending Egypt's exclusive rights to control the canal, which had long been overseen by the British. He began to speak of the Arab Nation and in defense of the Palestinian right of return.

War came suddenly in October when Israeli troops crossed their southwestern border and attacked Egyptian forces in the Sinai Peninsula, then moved toward the Suez Canal. British and French forces joined the fight on the Israeli side. But the United States and the Soviet Union—in rare agreement—demanded that Britain, France, and Israel withdraw. The two superpowers had separate interests in the region, but they prevailed. The withdrawal left Nasser in control of the Suez Canal. His popularity surged across the Arab world. He began talking about the importance of Palestine to all Arabs.

One day in the spring of 1957, Dalia was playing with her girlfriends after school. They were at a concrete shelter in Ramla, the same claustrophobic bunker where they'd practiced air-raid drills during the Suez crisis. Most of her friends had been lighter-skinned girls from Europe, but recently a new wave of olive- and brown-skinned children had arrived from Iraq, Egypt, Yemen, and other Arab countries. No longer welcome in the Arab world, these "Oriental Jews" (also known as Sephardic or *Mizrahi*) came to Israel for safe haven.

Among many of Dalia's classmates was a sense that the darkskinned schoolmates were "bringing the class down."

Dalia was stunned when a Polish friend stood atop the concrete shelter and, hands on hips, declared her intent to expel the darker Jews from their play group. There would now be two competing groups among the girls: a "black group" and a "white group." The other European girls murmured their agreement. Because of her light skin, the white group would include Dalia, who was also Sephardic, with roots in Spain.

The Polish girl threw a stone at a dark-skinned classmate, and Dalia stepped forward. "Where did you say you came from?" she asked the "white" group of girls. "And remind me, what happened to the Jews there?" She paused. "Of all people who should know better," she said. "Of all people who should know not to treat someone badly just because they are different. If you are going to have a black group and a white group, then I am going with the black group." The issue never rose again with her classmates.

That same year, Ahmad and Zakia Khairi moved their family back to Ramallah. They had received a family inheritance and would be able to buy a modest property in the West Bank and think about higher education for the children.

By then, Bashir had grown more serious, and mature beyond his years. More than ever, Bashir was focused on return. It would avenge the Palestinian defeat and restore his family's dignity. He viewed Egyptian president Nasser as a man who would unite the entire Arab world.

On the plane that took them back to Ramallah, Bashir's father fainted. "When we landed he was still in what now seemed like a coma," a family member recalled. "We hit his face to wake him. He did not wake up. The captain came in and said, 'It seems he is dead.'"

Bashir, who was fifteen years old, brought his face close to his father's and took his hand. "Yabba, wake up!"

Ahmad opened his eyes. "Yes, my son," he said. "What is it?"

The family would tell this story for years: Ahmad responded only to the voice of his firstborn son.

"This was the miracle of Bashir," his sister Khanom recalled.

Since the time Bashir and his family went into exile in Ramallah, moved to Gaza, and returned to Ramallah, tens of thousands of Jews had come to Israel from Arab countries. Many of these *Mizrahi* still lived in crude tent camps and shacks on the outskirts of Ramla and were desperate for work and better living conditions. They were discouraged from speaking Arabic or from listening to their beloved classical Arab music, especially with the rise of Nasser. The only work many of them could find was sweeping streets or "building" forests for the Jewish National Fund (JNF).

The forests, part of what the JNF called "total redemption of the land of Israel for the entire Jewish people," were part of a legacy of "BOULDER-STREWN mountains, stagnant swamps, hard, arid soil, and sterile sand dunes [that] must be redeemed from the neglect of twenty centuries." The forests in many cases were planted on land that had only recently held Arab villages. From 1948 until the mid-1960s, hundreds of villages were demolished—by bulldozers, by army units training demolition crews, and by aerial bombing—to be replaced by new cities, expanded kibbutzim, or JNF forests. The work of the *Mizrahi* and other immigrants for the JNF thus served several purposes: it eliminated the former residences of villagers who might attempt to "infiltrate" across the armistice lines; it cemented Israel's position against the UN resolution that authorized the return of Palestinian refugees; and it ensured low-paying work for thousands of poor Jewish immigrants from the Arab countries and elsewhere.

Like many of the early immigrants, the *Mizrahi* needed to feel they belonged in the Jewish state. The director of the Ramla office of the Israeli national labor federation worked to forge an Israeli identity out of the patchwork of nationalities and more than a dozen languages. He organized classes, plays, and concerts in Hebrew; evenings of folklore from Bulgaria, Morocco, and Yemen; and neighborhood culture and hiking clubs.

The model that was held up for all of the immigrants, especially the men, was the Sabra, the native-born Israeli whose optimism, strength, and mythical heroism was something to aspire toward. The Sabra was handsome, tough, physically strong, an ardent Zionist, upbeat, without fear, and unencumbered by the weakness of his ancestors.

For many new Israelis, this potent icon was something to strive for. They wore the Sabra "uniform"—khaki shorts and a khaki or faded blue work shirt and "biblical sandals." But for the older generation of immigrants, the Sabra image was often impossible to attain. For Holocaust survivors, it was absurd. For the Sabra, the Holocaust survivors often represented the shame of Jews going like sheep to the slaughter. Thus, Dalia recalled years later, the phrase *Never again* was not only a promise by Jews not to repeat the past; it also indicated a desire, rooted in shame, to distance themselves from the image of the victim.

Bulgarians were widely respected in Israel. They had none of what would come to be known as the "Holocaust complex." They gained a reputation as fair-minded and hardworking, with a passion for European high culture. Solia Eshkenazi embodied this, with her love of music and literature. But as Dalia grew older, she noticed how her mother would often speak of the winds that tumbled through the narrow corridors of her hometown in Bulgaria, or the hikes she and her friends used to take up Vitosha Mountain.

As a teenager, Dalia began to see her mother as an uprooted tree that couldn't take to new soil. Moshe had brought his skills with him to help build a new state, but Solia aged quickly. Her job in the tax office did not suit her personality and the radiance and mischief she'd arrived with. Her world had narrowed, and she grew quieter.

Dalia graduated from high school in 1966 and made plans to enroll at Tel Aviv University to study English literature. She'd taken a special English-language curriculum at an international high school in Yafo, now a mixed Arab-Jewish town just south of Tel Aviv. (Arabs still called the town Jaffa.) The Israeli army had recruited Dalia into its officers' training corps, a special program for gifted students that allowed them to attend college before their military service.

By the mid-1960s, Ramla—with its concrete smokestacks on the outskirts of town, its high percentage of unemployed *Mizrahi*, and its Arab "ghetto"—had gained a reputation across Israel as tough and gritty. But life had finally achieved some normality for Dalia and her fellow countrypeople. For most of her high school years, conflict with the Arabs had been relatively restrained, and she could afford not to think about it much. But then she noticed a change.

To the outside world, Israel had made it clear, once and for all, that it would never grant the Palestinian refugees the right of return. But as Nasser's strength grew with the rise of pan-Arab nationalism, threats emerged from the Arab Nationalist Movement and a new group, called the Palestine Liberation Organization (PLO). The relative quiet between Israel and the Arab world seemed doomed.

Dalia could sense it. Another war, it seemed, would be impossible to avoid.

Chapter 12
WAR

On Monday morning, June 5, 1967, Bashir Khairi stood before a judge in civil court, arguing a case on behalf of a client. Bashir was twenty-five and a recent graduate of Cairo University Law School, specializing in labor matters. The court had convened in Ramallah in the Jordanian-controlled West Bank, the territory King Abdullah had annexed to his kingdom seventeen years earlier. His grandson Hussein was now Jordan's king and head of state.

Ramallah had completely changed since the day in 1948 when Ahmad and Zakia had taken Bashir and the other children to Gaza. Gone was the desperation of a refugee population sleeping under the trees. Gone, too, were thousands of well-to-do Ramallans, mostly Christians, who had fled the West Bank for the United States in the years following the Nakba. At the edges of town stood the concrete dwellings and narrow, refuse-strewn lanes of the refugee camps. Each year the UN refugee agency was required to submit a budget for renewed funding. Receiving long-term funds or building more permanent-looking housing would imply a UN admission that the refugees were not going home. This position was still unacceptable for the "host" governments; the grassroots political factions that were based in the camps; and most of the refugees themselves. For Palestinians, resistance meant no compromise on the right of return, no matter how firm Israel's position.

Bashir, like most Palestinians, believed there was only one way the land would come back to his people. Force expelled us from our land, he reasoned, and only force will get it back.

Bashir faced the judge and made the case for his client. As he sat down, a young man darted through the courtroom door, strode swiftly to Bashir, and began whispering in his ear. It was a little before noon.

For nineteen years, Palestinian refugees had been waiting for the moment they would return to their homes. At first, they had thought this would happen in a matter of weeks. When Israel barred them from returning, hopes shifted to the UN resolution advocating the right of return. Years later, still in exile, the refugees began to put their faith in "armed struggle." Increasingly, they turned to Egypt's Nasser.

Bashir, while studying law in Cairo, was inspired by Nasser's dream of unifying the Arabs. Bashir's focus on return now had a vehicle, and he set aside all other personal ambitions. He believed his discipline would be rewarded, and his people delivered, by the heroic Nasser.

Nasser's nationalization of the Suez Canal, to the anger of the United States, Great Britain, France, and Israel, was a source of deep pride for Bashir and millions of others on the Arab streets. Unlike the UN resolutions on paper, Bashir believed, Nasser could end the long exile of the Palestinians by force of arms. Bashir and his fellow student activists in Cairo believed Arab unity was the key to return. Some students began training in secret "special forces" camps in Egypt and elsewhere. They learned how to plant mines and fire anti-tank weapons. They jumped from airplanes, waded through swamps, slept on hard ground, ate snakes, and went without food for days.

Two young men emerged from the growing guerrilla movement: Yasser Arafat and Khalil al-Wazir, known as Abu Jihad. They believed return would come only if it was led by an autonomous Palestinian political and military organization devoted to armed struggle. Neither Abu Jihad, who had been expelled from al-Ramla in 1948, nor Arafat trusted in the idea of deliverance coming from the other Arab states, which they believed had sold out the Palestinians in 1948. Together they founded the guerrilla group known as Fatah.

Throughout 1965 and 1966, Fatah launched a series of attacks from the West Bank and Lebanon on mostly isolated targets in Israel. The attacks sharply raised anxieties in the Jewish state. These attacks, and the Israeli reprisals, had drawn a reluctant King Hussein of Jordan deeper into the conflict.

On November 13, 1966, Israeli planes, tanks, and troops attacked the West Bank village of Samu, blowing up dozens of houses and killing twenty-one Jordanian soldiers. The massive scale of the invasions shocked even some supporters of Israel; U.S. officials immediately condemned the attack. U.S. president Lyndon B. Johnson assured King Hussein that his "disapproval of this action has been made known to the government of Israel in the strongest terms."

The king's fears of an Israeli occupation of the West Bank were secondary to his worries at home. The Samu attack badly damaged his position, and opponents argued that his policy of peaceful coexistence with Israel had been dictated by the U.S. and had failed. Pressure grew on the king to appear more militant toward Israel.

Waves of violent protest began against Hussein's regime. Palestinians accused the king of being weak and unprepared, and they demanded arms to fight Israel. A PLO broadcast from Cairo called on the Jordanian army to overthrow Hussein. Riots broke out in Jordan and the West Bank. The king imposed martial law.

Now the split in the Arab world became more obvious than ever: Egypt and its ally Syria stood in favor of "pan-Arab unity," while King Hussein was labeled a pro-Western "imperialist agent" and "ally of Zionism." Syria called for Hussein's overthrow, and Nasser declared that the king was "ready to sell the Arab nation in the same manner as Abdullah sold it in 1948."

Bashir stood firmly on the side of Nasser and the pan-Arab movement.

More tensions drove the region closer to war. In May, Nasser sent thousands of troops into Sinai toward the Israeli border, and he ordered UN peacekeeping troops out of Sinai. Israel began to mass thousands of its own troops along the border. Nasser announced the closing of the Straits of Tiran, declaring, "The Jews threaten us with war and we say to them, *Ahlan wa sahlan* [you are welcome]. We are ready!"

The Israelis saw this as a declaration of war.

In Ramla, Dalia unfurled the last square of black construction paper and taped it onto the window next to the other black squares. Now no light would escape. A day or two earlier, the police had stood on Herzl Street with brushes and cans of blue-black paint, stopping cars between Tel Aviv and Jerusalem and swabbing their headlights. Blackened headlights would still cast a dim path but not emit light that could be detected by enemy aircraft. Whether those jets would ever come, whether a single shot would ever be fired, no one knew. Across the country, Israelis were mobilizing: schools were turned into shelters as citizens and soldiers dug trenches, stepped up blood drives, prepared hospital beds, made plans to send their children to Europe, and dug ten thousand graves.

Dalia was nineteen years old, but during this "period of waiting" she often felt like crawling under a blanket. She had never felt like this, yet she understood that for others something terrible and familiar was reawakening. Later she would recall it as a "collective fear of annihilation." Her mother's face wore an expression of perpetual worry.

The radio picked up a broadcast of a serene Egyptian voice, saying, "Why don't you go back to where you came from? You don't stand a chance."

Dalia knew that the Israeli army, in whose officers' training corps program she now served, was strong. But in a community where Holocaust survivors still were walking around with numbers on their arms, Dalia believed "one had to take sick fantasies seriously." She was petrified, and so were her parents and her aunts.

Officials in U.S. President Johnson's administration were trying to keep Israel from attacking Egypt, while assessing whether Nasser truly wanted war. The U.S. assessment was that the Egyptian forces in the Sinai were "defensive in character" and were not preparing to invade Israel. U.S. officials also believed that Israel would win any conflict against its Arab enemies and could "maintain internal security, defend successfully against simultaneous Arab attacks on all fronts, launch limited attacks simultaneously on all fronts, or hold onto any three fronts while mounting successfully a major offensive on the fourth." The assessment declared that Israel's capabilities were enhanced because "the Arab states are hampered by a lack of cohesiveness and by friction among Arab leaders."

King Hussein of Jordan, feeling increasingly isolated, decided that without an alliance with Nasser, Jordan would be vulnerable to attacks from Israel, or from Palestinians within his own kingdom who would see his inaction as a betrayal of the Arab cause. He agreed to place the forces of his Arab Legion, along with Iraqi, Syrian, and Saudi troops, under the command of an Egyptian general. Palestinians were elated. Upon his return from Cairo, adoring throngs hoisted the king's car and carried it along the street.

Meanwhile, American officials considered sending a U.S.- and British-led convoy of Western ships through the Strait of Tiran as a signal to Nasser that all nations, including Israel, should enjoy free passage. U.S. generals objected, believing that if an American ship drew fire, the result would be war—only this time, the U.S. would be directly involved. In a world dominated by two nuclear superpowers— the U.S. and the Soviet Union—there was no telling where that might lead. The convoy plan was pulled.

Nasser claimed that he had no intentions of attacking Israel, but also that he would not back down from his position on the Strait of Tiran. He wrote to U.S. president Johnson to explain his reasoning: "An aggressive armed force was able to oust that people [of Palestine] from their country and reduce them to refugees on the borders of their homeland. Today the forces of aggression impede the Arab people's established right of return. . . . I may ask how far any government is able to control the feelings of more than one million Palestinians who for twenty years, the international community—whose responsibility herein is inescapable—has failed to secure their return to their homeland. The UN General Assembly merely confirms that right, at every session."

Nasser privately expressed his preference for a peaceful solution, but to the rest of the world the voices coming out of Cairo seemed certain of war and confident of victory. Nasser challenged Israel "to try all your weapons. Put them to the test, they will spell Israel's death and annihilation."

To Bashir and his family, words like these meant the enemy would be vanquished and the family would return home. To Dalia and her family, the words meant what they said—annihilation.

Nasser's words amounted to a monumental gamble. And he was in for the surprise of his life. At 7:45 a.m. on June 5, French-built Israeli bombers roared out of their bases and crossed into Egyptian airspace. Fifteen minutes later, tanks and infantry moved into Gaza and toward the Sinai frontier. The war with Egypt had begun. Israel took no action at that hour against Jordan, Iraq, or Syria, but warned that any hostile action from Jordan would be reacted to "with all our might."

A few hours later, Bashir stood up in the Ramallah courtroom and called to the judge: "Your honor!" he bellowed. "I have just received word that the war has begun."

The judge halted the proceedings. Bashir hurried home. On the streets, people were dashing in and out of shops, stocking up on canned food, candles, and kerosene. Others waited in long lines outside the flour mills. On the sidewalks, men crowded around tables beneath overhead speakers, straining to hear the radio. The city was expectant, not only of war, but of the annual throngs of summer visitors that would flock there after the victory. Nineteen years after the Nakba had transformed Ramallah, the city had again become a summer haven for the Arab world, with twenty-one hotels and an annual music festival attended by families from Libya to Kuwait. During high season the restaurants would stay open until 2:00 a.m. and reopen two hours later. Now it seemed the revelers would mark a more profound celebration: Palestine would again be in the hands of the Arabs.

At home, Bashir found Ahmad, Zakia, Nuha, and his other siblings transfixed before the radio. Egyptian aircraft had shot down three-quarters of the attacking Israeli jets, according to a report from Cairo. Egyptian troops had taken the offensive in Sinai, and Jordan had captured a strategic hill in Jerusalem. But this "news" was fake; the Egyptians had won nothing.

"We thought victory was in our hands," Bashir would say thirty-seven years later. "That we would be victorious and we would be going back home. . . . Sorry to say, that was not the case. It was an illusion."

Chapter 13
SIX HOURS

In truth, Nasser's entire air force lay smoking on the tarmacs in Cairo, Sinai, and the Nile delta. Israel's surprise attack had destroyed virtually all of Egypt's Soviet-built fighter jets, and now the Jewish state had the sky over Sinai all to itself.

To make matters worse, Jordanian analysts misread intense radar activity as Egyptian jets on the attack, not Israeli fighters returning to their base to refuel. Invoking a mutual defense pact, the commander in chief of the Egyptian forces authorized a Jordanian offensive against Israel.

King Hussein had assurances from Israel that it would not attack Jordan first and warning of the consequences if Jordan fired the first shot. The king, however, was bound to the pact with Egypt. So Jordanian forces began firing long-range artillery toward Israeli suburbs near Tel Aviv and an airfield. Fifteen minutes later, Jordanian howitzers fired thousands of shells on neighborhoods and military targets in Jerusalem. Jordanian, Syrian, and Iraqi fighter jets sliced into Israeli airspace as Jordanian infantry churned forward toward Israeli positions.

"Brother Arabs everywhere," stated a broadcast from Jordan, "the enemy this morning has launched an aggression on our Arab land and airspace."

"The Zionist barracks in Palestine," declared a radio report from Cairo, "is about to be destroyed."

Such triumphal messages would have thrilled Bashir's family and terrified Dalia's. But the facts told a different story. By midafternoon, the air forces of Jordan, Syria, Iraq, and Egypt had all been demolished. The Six-Day War was essentially decided on its first day, June 5, 1967, in six hours.

Bashir could hear explosions. The headquarters of the Jordanian army in Ramallah was crumbling under Israeli fire. Then the city's main radio transmitter went down in another series of thunderous booms.

Bashir and his family assumed these attacks would soon be answered and that reinforcements—Iraqis or more troops from Jordan—would fortify the city. Surely the Arabs understood the strategic importance of Ramallah, a key transport hub and center of West Bank communications. Soon, however, there were reports of Jordanian troops being wiped out when they tried to reach Jerusalem, as fighter jets obliterated an entire infantry battalion. It wasn't clear where reinforcements for Ramallah might be coming from. Bashir listened to the explosions through the night and into the next day, shaking the city and its confidence.

The concentrated attack left Arab forces virtually destroyed. Command headquarters was left with a series of terrible choices: they could cease fire, retreat, or fight for one more day in the West Bank, "resulting in the isolation and destruction of the entire Jordanian army." Nasser urged the Jordanian army to vacate the West Bank while Arab leaders pressed for a cease-fire.

In the light of the early evening of June 6, Bashir stood on the roof of an apartment building in Ramallah, facing south. It was warm and clear but for the dark pillars of smoke rising from the direction of Jerusalem and the haze around the Mount of Olives just to the east.

Bashir squinted through the smoke, out past the refugee camp and toward the tower of the airstrip where he'd landed coming from Gaza ten years earlier. There he could see a line of tanks and jeeps moving north. As news of the approaching troops reached the streets below, some Palestinians began preparing to greet them. They assumed they would be Iraqi reinforcements.

Bashir remained on the roof, his left hand characteristically in his pocket, and fixed his gaze on the road to the south. Slowly, as the tanks came closer, he surmised that they were not Iraqi.

Ramallah fell that night as Israeli ground forces moved in. There was little resistance; eyewitnesses would say that many Jordanian troops had retreated well before the Israelis arrived.

By late that evening, Dalia knew that the war was won. She experienced it not with elation—not yet, since the fighting was still going on—but rather with a sense that a miracle was taking place in Israel. *How could this have happened?* she thought. *Did God save us? How can this be?*

With the news the previous day that Israel had destroyed Arab air forces, Dalia felt a profound relief such as she had never experienced, just as before the war she had felt such horror. For her parents, the feeling tapped something old, from twenty years earlier: the moment when they learned that the Bulgarian authorities had suspended the deportation orders for the Jews and that they would not be boarding trains for Poland.

By June 10, the war was officially over. Israel had captured the West Bank, the Gaza Strip, East Jerusalem, the Golan Heights, and the Egyptian Sinai Peninsula. The United Nations imposed a cease-fire, and the shooting and shelling stopped. Dalia and her family began jumping wildly, laughing and hugging and kissing one another.

Dalia started to dance: slowly at first, arms extended, neck tilted, head back, eyes half-open, loose skirt shifting softly around her. She spun between the walls of Jerusalem stone. Gradually the other women joined Dalia, and they formed a circle, hands on one another's shoulders, moving to the *hora*, the Israeli national dance. They swayed through the open house, out to the yard, past the jacaranda tree and the lemon tree, laughing and weeping.

Dalia would always remember this night and its abiding sense of miracle and liberation.

Within a week, thousands of refugees began arriving in Ramallah. They'd been ordered from their homes; those who tried to return were blocked by a line of tanks and soldiers shooting in the air. In all, more than two hundred thousand Palestinians were displaced by the war.

Life was transformed. The summer theater festival and countless other plans were canceled abruptly. Israeli soldiers took the place of Jordanian police, and the prisons began to fill with young Palestinian men.

Authorities soon announced a new justice system to be administered by occupation judges in the West Bank. But the Israelis had a problem: Almost no Arab lawyers would come to court, rendering the new Israeli courts virtually silent and empty. They were on strike and the action had been organized, the Israeli authorities would soon learn, by a young West Bank lawyer named Bashir Khairi.

Bashir and other organizers were threatened with jail time and enticed with a promise of reduced sentences for clients already in prison. One judge told Bashir he'd release fifteen Palestinians accused of illegal demonstrations if Bashir simply showed up in court to represent them.

"As long as there's an Israeli flag behind the judge in the courtroom, I won't be representing my people," Bashir said.

In the days after the war, the Arab states would publicly declare "no reconciliation, no negotiation, no recognition" regarding Israel, but these were increasingly taken as empty words by Palestinians. Strangely, as the occupation wore on, a sense of calm and clarity came over Bashir. The loss was devastating, but it made one thing clear: Palestinians could rely only on themselves to deliver their own justice. The right of return, guaranteed by the United Nations, would never be delivered by the UN or the international community. Bashir and his people would go back to their homeland only through the sweat and blood of armed struggle.

Thousands of young Palestinian men signed up to become *fedayeen*—freedom fighters, or, literally, "those who sacrifice." Their goal was to guarantee the right of return by any means necessary. Yasser Arafat, Abu Jihad, and members of Fatah began launching small raids into Israel again. The attacks had little practical effect, but they were significant on a psychological level—rattling the Israeli population, for whom safety and security were paramount.

Chapter 14
THE FIRST ENCOUNTER

B ashir stood with his two cousins at the gate of the stone home in al-Ramla. How many times, he wondered, had his mother, Zakia, walked through this same gate? How many times had his father, Ahmad, passed by, coming home tired from work, rapping his knuckles on the front door in the special knock he always gave to announce his arrival?

Bashir reached for the bell and pressed it.

Dalia Eshkenazi, jolted from her contemplation, walked from the veranda to the front door. She picked up a large key and trotted lightly down the path to the metal gate.

"*Rak rega*—just a moment," Dalia called, using both hands to raise the heavy key to the lock. She opened the gate partway and looked out between the gate and the pillar.

Three men were standing there stiffly in coats and ties, in the stifling Israeli summer heat. The men appeared to be in their twenties. Dalia knew immediately that they were Arabs.

"*Ken?*" she said. "Yes?"

The men looked uncomfortable, as if they didn't know what to say now that Dalia had asked them their business. For a moment they remained quiet, but Dalia knew why they had come.

"As soon as I saw them," she remembered, "I felt, *Wow, it's them.* It was as if I'd always been waiting for them."

Now, the youngest one, the one with the thin face and large brown eyes, opened his mouth.

"This was my father's house," said the young man in his halting English. "And I lived here, too."

Dalia was ready for what came next.

"Would it be possible," the young man asked, "for us to come in and see the house?"

Dalia knew she had very little time to process this question and respond. Logic dictated she tell the men to come back when she wasn't alone. If she allowed them to come in, what would that be inviting? The Six-Day War had ended just a few weeks before.

Bashir gazed at the woman. She hadn't responded to his question. Fresh in his mind was the terrible reception Yasser had received at his childhood home only an hour earlier. At least Ghiath, his other cousin, had seen his old house, the one now converted to a school for Israeli children. This young woman, whoever she was, seemed to be taking her time.

Dalia looked at the three young men. They were quiet and apprehensive. She knew that if she told them to come back later, she might never see them again. Yet if she opened the door, she might not be able to close it. So many thoughts were rushing through her head.

"Yes," Dalia said finally. She smiled broadly. "Please, come in."

Bashir looked at the striking young woman with short dark hair. She was smiling at him, holding open the metal gate.

"Please, come in," Bashir thought he heard the woman say. He watched as she turned to walk up the stone path toward the house.

Was this possible? Bashir looked at his cousins. Had the Israeli woman really said to follow her? He stood at the gate, frozen, doubting everything. The men remained planted there as the woman disappeared into the house.

Bashir looked at Yasser. "I am sure she said, 'You are welcome,'" he told his cousin. A moment later, the woman's head appeared again in the doorway. She was looking at them quizzically.

"Are you sure we can come in?" Bashir managed in his stiff English.

"Yes." The woman laughed. "Please, come up the path."

Bashir would later recall stepping gingerly, from one stone to the next, taking care not to crush the grass growing between them. He turned back to his cousins, who were still immobile at the gate. "Follow me," he said to Yasser and Ghiath. "Come into my house."

Dalia stood in the doorway, still smiling as the men came up the path. She knew it was not advisable in the wake of war for a young Israeli woman to invite three Arab men inside her house. This prospect, however, did not unnerve her in the least. Dalia had sensed a vulnerability in these young men, and she was certain they had no intention of harming her. She felt safe.

"Please, give me five minutes," Dalia told the men. "Only five minutes." She wanted the inside of the home to look nice, so that her visitors would have a good image of the house and the people living in it.

Bashir barely heard her. He was taking in the garden: purple and red flowers shaped like candles and closed against the sun; the flowers of the *fitna* tree his mother had told him about, exploding from the branches in brilliant white and yellow; deep red roses from abundant bushes.

Behind the house stood a palm tree, its gray tufts rising into broad green leaves far above the roof. In the backyard, he hoped, the lemon tree would still be standing.

Bashir fixed his gaze on the wooden front door, the one his father had always knocked on when he came home from work, announcing his arrival and bursting through the door as Bashir raced toward him.

What was taking the woman so long? It seemed much longer than five minutes. Could she be calling the police? The cousins grew increasingly wary.

Bashir could see the white Jerusalem stone his father had laid with his own hands thirty-one years earlier. If he were standing a bit closer, Bashir could have run his fingertips along its cratered surface, its miniature hills and valleys like the landscape of Palestine itself.

"You can come inside now," the woman said as she reappeared in the doorway. "You are welcome. Come in, feel at home." It was a universal welcome—Make yourself at home—yet these particular words seemed especially strange to Bashir as he approached the front door.

The cousins crossed the threshold: Bashir first, followed by Yasser and Ghiath. Bashir took a few careful steps and looked around, standing in silence, breathing in the air of the large open room, exhaling, breathing in again. It was much as he had pictured it: spare and clean. He would recall feeling as if he were in a mosque; as if he, Bashir, were a holy man.

Dalia would recall leading the cousins through each room, wanting them to feel welcome and comfortable. After the initial tour, she told them to take their time and experience the house as they wished. She withdrew, watching them with fascination.

Bashir looked like he was in a trance. He floated down hallways and in and out of doorways, touching tile, glass, wood, and painted plaster walls, absorbing the feel of every surface.

"And I had a sense that they were walking in a temple, in silence," Dalia remembered many years later. "And that every step meant so much to them."

Bashir stopped in front of the open door to a small bedroom in a corner of the house, near the backyard. He could hear Dalia's voice behind him. "This is my bedroom," she said.

"Yes," Bashir said. "And it was mine."

Dalia looked up at the wall above her bed. On it she had tacked a picture of a beaming, blue-eyed Israeli soldier from a cover of *Life* magazine—the archetype of the Israeli Sabra. The soldier was standing chest high in the Suez Canal, his Uzi submachine gun thrust above his head at the end of the Six-Day War. To Dalia the image stood for liberation, for warding off a threat, and for survival. Standing with Bashir in the doorway to the bedroom, she suddenly realized that Bashir might see that poster differently.

Bashir would recall Dalia saying, "I think you left the house when you were very young. Maybe the same year we came."

Bashir wanted to explode, to yell, *We didn't "leave" the house! You forced us out!* Instead he said, "We haven't been properly introduced. My name is Bashir Khairi. And these are my cousins Ghiath and Yasser."

Dalia introduced herself and told them she was on summer vacation from Tel Aviv University. She took care not to tell them she was in the officers' training corps for the Israel Defense Forces. This was partly because they were Arabs and she was a Jew; it was also because she felt, welling up within her, a surge of *akhrayut*:

responsibility, or, literally, an ability to respond to another person. Questions from her childhood returned: What was an Arab house? Who had lived here before? Why did they leave? She realized that these three would have answers.

Dalia thought, *Finally I have opened a door that has so long been closed.* She would recall this moment as the beginning of her quest toward understanding.

"And now," Dalia said, "will you allow me to treat you as guests? May I offer you something to drink?"

As guests, Bashir thought. *Should a person be a guest in his own house?* "I don't mind at all," he said quickly to Dalia. "Yes, thank you."

"Let's sit in the garden," Dalia said, pointing toward the backyard. "It's very beautiful. What would you like? Lemonade? Turkish coffee?"

The three cousins sat in the sun in the garden. Bashir's eyes were like the lens of a camera, taking in the exterior walls, window frames, roofline. He recorded soil, sand, branches, leaves, fruit. He even recorded the blades of grass growing out between the layers of stone on the house. Now his eyes rested on the lemon tree, standing in the corner of the garden.

"I don't think they changed anything in the house," Yasser said.

"Only the furniture," Bashir replied.

Dalia came with the drinks—Bashir later remembered small cups of Turkish coffee; Dalia is certain she served lemonade. "I hope this visit gave you some rest," she said, placing small china cups and saucers—or perhaps it was the glasses of lemonade—before each cousin.

"Of course, of course," Bashir said.

They made quiet small talk and listened to one another sip. After a few minutes, Yasser stood up. "I think it's time to go," he said. But Bashir wasn't quite ready.

"Could you give me permission to have another look at the house?" he asked Dalia.

She answered with a smile. "Of course! Feel at home."

Bashir looked at Yasser. "I'm going to go for just a minute," he said.

A few minutes later, Dalia and Bashir were facing each other again at the gate. "I hope we will meet again," said Dalia.

"Yes, of course, Dalia," Bashir said. "I hope to see you again. And one day you must come to visit us in Ramallah."

"How will I know where to find you?"

"When you arrive in Ramallah, ask anyone," said Bashir. "They will show you to my home."

On the bus ride back, the cousins sat as before, one behind the other. They rode east in silence, exhausted. They had seen their houses, but now what? Bashir gazed out the window at nothing, aware of a new burden resting like stones on his chest.

When he reached his house, Bashir climbed the concrete steps. He opened the door and found his sisters and brothers, his father, and his mother all waiting for the returning traveler. Ahmad sat in the middle, in a chair at the kitchen table.

Bashir couldn't bear the scene. "I am very tired," he said. "The way was long and the story is longer. Let me rest first, and tomorrow I will tell you everything." It was only 6:00 p.m.

"Sleep, my son," Ahmad said, his eyes watering. "Sleep, *habibi*, my dear son."

In the morning the family was waiting. Bashir took his time, recounting every moment of the journey with his cousins. Everyone pumped Bashir with questions—everyone, that is, except Ahmad, who remained quiet while the others demanded a replay of Bashir's every step, his every touch of stone. Did the light still stream in through the south windows in the afternoon? Were the pillars on the gate still standing straight? Was the front gate still painted olive green? Was the paint chipping? "If it still is," Zakia said, "when you go back you can bring a can of paint to make it new again, Bashir; you can bring shears and cut the grass growing up along the stone path. How is the lemon tree, does it look nice? Did you bring the fruit? . . . You didn't? Did you rub the leaves and smell them, did your fingers smell like fresh-cut lemons? How were the stones of the house, were they still cool and rough to the touch? . . . What else, Bashir, what else? Please don't leave anything out."

Throughout the questions, Ahmad had been as still as a mountain, his eyes watering. Abruptly he stood, pushing back his chair. Tears streaked his face as he left the kitchen and walked down the hallway. All eyes followed Ahmad, but no one dared call him back. He closed the bedroom door.

"God forgive you, my son," Zakia said. "You have opened our wounds again."

Chapter 15
LONGING

By September 1967, the lawyers' strike showed no signs of waning. Bashir and his fellow attorneys dug in, using the strike to protest both the occupation of the West Bank and the recent annexation of East Jerusalem by Israel. The annexation carried a huge professional and financial impact on the lawyers. They faced permanent loss of work, or, at the very least, the necessity to learn Hebrew and pass the Israeli bar exam. Bashir and the others had no intention of doing so. That would have implied acceptance.

Bashir believed the occupation was temporary and that soon he would be getting back to work. But signs suggested otherwise: already some Israelis were building settlements in the West Bank.

Late in the evening of September 17, Bashir woke to the sounds of men yelling and fists pounding on the door. "The Israeli soldiers are surrounding the house!" someone screamed.

Ten soldiers in battle gear stood at the door when Bashir opened it, with machine guns pointed at his chest.

"All of you bring your identification," a soldier shouted. Bashir brought his ID and the soldier looked him over. "You're Bashir," he said. "Get dressed and come with me."

Bashir spent one hundred days in a Ramallah jail, where he was interrogated about his activism. "You are a leader," he was told. "Give us details about the resistance."

Each time, Bashir's reply was the same. "I believe in one thing: Palestine. And I hate one thing: occupation. And if you want to punish me, do it."

Bashir's arrest was part of a much wider counterinsurgency designed to root out dissidents, guerrillas, and others suspected of plotting attacks on Israeli soil.

Signs of accommodation with Israel were already emerging from the Arab states. As Bashir sat in jail, a close associate of Egyptian president Nasser wrote a series of articles calling for a Palestinian state in the West Bank and Gaza, suggesting that the return to old Palestine would not happen. The UN adopted a new resolution calling for "withdrawal of Israeli armed forces from territories occupied in the recent conflict" in exchange for Arab recognition of Israel. The boundaries would be far different from those outlined in the 1947 partition plan. Israel would control 78 percent of historic Palestine, including al-Ramla and Lydda.

Nasser and King Hussein signaled that they would support the new resolution. Yasser Arafat's goal of a mass insurgency was fading, but a new independence movement emerged. The Popular Front for the Liberation of Palestine attacked Israel's national airport.

Bashir was released from jail at the end of 1967. No formal charges were filed. As he walked free, he would remember later, "I loved Palestine more than ever, and I hated occupation more than ever."

One clammy gray morning in January 1968, Dalia awoke in Ramla with Bashir and his family on her mind. For months she had been thinking about his invitation to visit him in Ramallah. Today, she hoped, would be the day. Dalia didn't have Bashir's address or telephone number, so she had no choice but to show up in person. She remembered that Bashir had told her, "When you get to Ramallah, just ask for the house of Bashir Khairi. Everyone will know."

A friend drove Dalia east toward what she called the Judean Hills. They splashed through potholes in the unpaved winter roads of the West Bank. Dalia knew that somewhere on these roads Israeli tanks and jeeps were on patrol, but she mostly saw a terrain of stony hills, olive groves, and ancient villages growing out of the landscape.

They drove on, traveling down strange and deserted roads in the Israeli-occupied West Bank, unsure of where they were going.

In Ramallah, it was just as Bashir had said. Dalia's friend pulled the car up near Manara Square in the heart of the town and Dalia asked a man on the street for the house of Bashir Khairi. The man knew who Bashir was and where he lived. Within minutes, Dalia and her friend were standing at the base of a concrete stairway as a neighbor went up to notify Bashir of his arriving guests.

Bashir, a few weeks removed from an Israeli jail, was in his room when his younger brother Kamel burst in. (Kamel had met Dalia when he accompanied his brother on a second visit to the house.) "Guess who's here?" Kamel asked excitedly. Bashir knew immediately. He bounded down the stairway to the street. There was Dalia, looking a little nervous.

It was cold, and dark skies threatened more rain. "I don't know if it's safe for you to visit," Bashir said. "Because I've just come out of prison."

"Why were you in prison?" Dalia asked.

"Because I love my country," Bashir replied.

Funny, Dalia thought. *I also love my country, and I haven't been imprisoned.* But she realized that Bashir was trying to protect her. He was being watched, and if Dalia went upstairs, she would risk surveillance, too. The irony was that Bashir was trying to shield Dalia from the eyes of her own army, of which she was now a part. She was faced with a decision, and she came to it quickly: she would not allow anyone to tell her whom she could or could not see. She looked at Bashir's thin, clean-shaven face and his large brown eyes. "Please," she said. "Let us have a visit."

Upstairs, Bashir led Dalia and her friend to an overstuffed couch in a cold, darkened living room. Bashir's sisters darted about, turning on lamps and preparing the room for the surprise guests. This was the first time Dalia had seen West Bank women, just as she imagined it was their first look at an Israeli not in uniform.

Bashir introduced his mother, Zakia, who greeted Dalia warmly, and within moments, Dalia would remember, "things suddenly began appearing on the table: teas, cakes, date pastries, Arabic sweets, Turkish coffee . . ." She was overwhelmed by the hospitality.

As warm as the family was, Dalia was struck by how temporary their home felt. Something central was missing. Dalia couldn't identify it precisely, but she felt as if the whole family were sitting on their suitcases.

"So," Bashir began in his hesitant English, "how are you, Dalia? How is your family? How are you doing in school?"

"I am fine," Dalia said. "Fine."

There was a pause.

Bashir regarded Dalia. He was content to let her determine the course of their conversation. After all, she was his guest. "You are welcome here, Dalia," he said. "I hope you will spend a nice day with us. You are generous and very nice to us."

All of the family eventually came out to greet Dalia, except for Bashir's father, Ahmad. Apparently, he wasn't home.

Dalia took another deep breath. She hesitated before posing the question but reminded herself that she had come to Ramallah for the opportunity to learn their story. "Bashir," she said, leaning forward, "I know this is a sensitive issue. . . . It must be very difficult that someone now is living in your house."

Bashir would have been content to let the conversation remain on the level of "How are you?" His sense of Arab hospitality dictated that he not challenge a visitor. This, however, was extraordinary. Dalia needed and deserved to be engaged in conversation.

"Listen, Dalia," Bashir said slowly. "How would you feel to leave your home, all your belongings, your entire spirit, in one place? Would you not fight to get it back with everything you have?"

There were many more details Bashir could have conveyed. He could have told Dalia what he and his family had experienced: about the Israeli army attacking Lydda and occupying al-Ramla in 1948; about the soldiers' rifle butts pounding on doors the next day; about the forced exile of tens of thousands of people; about the nineteen years of inconsolable longing for home; about the willingness to fight, by any means necessary, for return. Instead, he stood up suddenly.

"Come, Dalia," Bashir said. "Let me show you something."

Dalia followed Bashir to a glass cabinet.

"Look at the cabinet and tell me what you see," Bashir said.

"Is this a test?"

"It is a test. Please tell me what you see in the cabinet."

"Books, vases, a picture of Abdel Nasser. Maybe some things hiding behind. And a lemon."

"You won," Bashir said. "Do you remember the lemon?"

"What about it? Is there a story?"

"Do you remember when I and my brother came to visit? . . . Yes? Do you remember that Kamel asked you for something as we left? And what you gave him as a gift?"

Dalia was silent for a moment. "Oh, my god. It's one of the lemons from that visit. But why did you keep it? It has been almost four months now."

They walked back to the living room. "To us this lemon is more than fruit, Dalia," Bashir said. "It is land and history. It is the window that we open to look at our history. A few days after we brought the lemon home, it was night, and I heard a movement in the house. I was asleep. I got up, and I was listening. We were so nervous when the occupation started. Even the movement of the trees used to wake us. And leave us worried. I heard the noise, and I got up. The noise was coming from this room right here. Do you know what I saw? My father, who is nearly blind."

"Yes," said Dalia. She was listening intently.

"Dalia, I saw him holding the lemon with both hands. And he was pacing back and forth in the room, and there were tears running down his cheeks."

"What did you do?"

"I went back to my room, sat on my bed, and I started thinking. Then I started talking to myself until the morning. And I understood why I love him so much."

Dalia was on the verge of tears herself. "What would happen if your father came to the house in Ramla?" she asked.

"He might have a breakdown. He always says he'd have a heart attack before he got to the door."

"And your mother?"

"My mother, too. She entered the house when she was a bride. And she gave birth in it, too." Bashir himself had been born in that house, twenty-six years earlier.

"We can see ourselves in you, Bashir," Dalia said. "We can remember our own history of exile over thousands of years. I can understand your longing for home because of our own experience of exile." Dalia was deeply moved and believed she was connecting with her new friend.

Bashir had never been able to understand how another people's ancient longing—their wish to return home from a millennial exile—could somehow be equated with the actual life of generations of Palestinians who lived and breathed in this land, who grew food from it, who buried their parents and grandparents in it. He was skeptical that this longing for Zion had much to do with Israel's creation.

"Israel first came to the imagination of the Western occupying powers for two reasons," he said.

"And what are they?" Dalia asked, now feeling her own skepticism grow.

"First, to get rid of you in Europe. Second, to rule the East through this government and to keep down the whole Arab world. And then the leaders started remembering the Torah and started to talk about the land of milk and honey, and the Promised Land."

"But there is good reason for this," Dalia objected. "And the reason is to protect us from being persecuted in other countries. To protect us from being slaughtered in cold blood just because we are Jews. I know the truth, Bashir. I know that my people were killed, slaughtered, put in gas ovens. Israel was the only safe place for us. It was the place where the Jews could finally feel that being a Jew is not a shame!"

"But you are saying that the whole world did this," Bashir replied. "It is not true. The Nazis killed the Jews. And we hate them. But why should we pay for what they did? Our people welcomed the Jewish people during the Ottoman Empire. They came to us, running away from Europeans, and we welcomed them with all that we had. We took care of them. But now because you want to live in a safe place, other people live in pain. If we take your family, for example. You come running from another place. Where should you stay? In a house that is owned by someone else? Will you take the house from them? And the owners—us—should we leave our house and go to another place? Is it justice that we should be expelled from our cities, our villages, our streets?"

Bashir continued: "We have history here—in Lydda, Haifa, Jaffa, al-Ramla. Many Jews who came here believed they were a people without a land going to a land without people. That is ignoring the indigenous people of this land. Their civilization, their history, their heritage, their culture. And now we are strangers. Strangers in every place. Why did this happen, Dalia? The Zionism did this to *you*, not just to the Palestinians."

For Dalia, the love of Zion was not something she felt she could explain quickly. "For two thousand years we were praying three times a day to return to this land," she told Bashir. "We tried to live in other places. But we realized we were not wanted in other places. We had to come back home."

The two young people stared at each other in silence.

"Okay, Bashir. I live in your home," Dalia said finally. "And this is also my home. It is the only home I know. So, what shall we do?"

"You can go back where you came from," Bashir said calmly.

Dalia felt as if Bashir had dropped a bomb. She wanted to scream, but she forced herself to listen.

"We believe that only those who came here before 1917"—the beginning of the British Mandate in Palestine—"have a right to be here. But anyone who came after 1917 cannot stay."

Dalia was astounded. "Well, since I was born and came here after 1917, that is no solution for me!" She was struck by the total contradiction of her situation: complete disagreement across a seemingly unbridgeable gulf, combined with the establishment of a bond through a common history, in a house where she felt utterly protected and welcomed. At the base of it, Dalia felt the depth of the Khairis' gratitude to her simply for having opened the door to the house in Ramla.

"This was an amazing situation to be in," Dalia recalled later. "That everybody could feel the warmth and the reality of our people meeting, meeting the other, and it was real, it was happening, and we were admiring each other's *being*, so to speak. And it was so tangible. And on the other hand, we were conversing of things that seemed *totally mutually exclusive*. That my life here is at *their* expense, and if they want to realize their dream, it's at *my* expense."

Dalia looked straight at Bashir. "I have nowhere else to go," she said. "I am staying here. The best thing is for you to live and leave us to live, too. We have to live together. We have to accept each other."

Bashir stared calmly at his new friend. "You are living in a place that does not belong to you, Dalia," he said. "This is my country. We were driven out of it."

"Well, you realize it is also my country," Dalia insisted.

"No, it's not. It's not your country. You stole it from us."

Dalia felt the word *stole* as a slap. She sat on the couch, insulted and aggravated. "You are leaving us in the sea," she finally said. "So what do you propose for us? Where shall we go?"

"I'm very sorry, but it is not my problem," Bashir said quietly. "The solution, Dalia, is very hard. When you plant a tree and it's not the place for it to live, it's not going to grow." He repeated his idea that Jews born outside of what was now Israel should go back to their homeland of origin.

Dalia could hardly believe this was a serious idea. "No, Bashir, no; we don't have anywhere to go back to."

"Yes, you can; it can be arranged. You'd be welcomed back."

"Bashir," Dalia said, leaning forward, "don't try to fix one wrong with another wrong! You want to turn us, again, into refugees?" *What am I doing here?* she thought. *What is the point of continuing this conversation?*

Still, Dalia had noticed that Bashir never repeated the threats of the Palestinian nationalists to one day take all of Palestine by force. He had never said, *We* will *take your house from you*—and Dalia had avoided asking him about his intentions or political affiliations. Each had chosen to reside within the contradiction: they were enemies, and they were friends. Therefore, Dalia believed, they had a reason to keep talking; the conversation itself was worth protecting.

Dalia stood up and said that it was time for her to go. She reached for Bashir's hand. "Really, I enjoyed spending time with you. And I feel that every time I understand more and more."

Bashir's mother and sisters came in, and Dalia thanked them.

"You are not just a guest in this house, Dalia," Bashir said. "You must come again and again, and we're going to do this, too."

Dalia turned as she reached the door. "I'm only one person searching for the truth," she said. "And I found the thread that's going to take me there."

Chapter 16
EXPLOSION

The morning of February 21, 1969, was dry and cold in Jerusalem. Israel Gefen, a veteran of World War II and three Arab-Israeli wars, was running an errand for his wife, a Canadian journalist. Gefen walked into a Supersol market just after 10:30 a.m. As he strode past the checkout counters and toward the coolers in the back, he noticed two young men speaking English in what he took to be South African accents. That was the last thing his mind recorded before the boom.

As he was thrown upward, as the force of the blast catapulted him back-first through the false ceiling and into the light fixtures overhead, Gefen knew that the explosion had come from a bomb.

He slammed hard onto the supermarket floor and saw the two young men, lifeless on the floor. Beside them a woman lay near death. A fourth victim lay on the floor nearby.

Gefen looked down at his left leg to see blood spurting from an artery near his ankle. A seeping red patch, the sign of another wound, was growing larger, oozing from his trousers. He pressed his fingers into his groin, putting firm pressure on the femoral artery at the top of his left leg, to stop the flow of blood. His ankle was nearly severed at the foot.

Gefen looked around. Smoke and dust were settling; the false ceiling dangled from above; and light fixtures, metal tins, and shattered plastic bottles lay amid pools of blood. He noticed the familiar wartime smell of gunpowder.

Two men emerged through the smoke and hurried Gefen outside and into a barber's chair next door. After two or three minutes, one of the men reappeared and helped Gefen into the cab of his pickup truck, and they raced through the streets of West Jerusalem.

"Talk to me," Gefen told the terrified driver as he darted through red lights, honking constantly and dodging buses, cars, and pedestrians. Gefen wanted the man to keep him awake; if he passed out, his hand would slip from his groin and the loss of blood would probably kill him.

A few minutes later, they arrived at a hospital entrance. Medics surrounded Gefen and wheeled him toward the emergency ward. It was strange, Gefen thought before passing out: he hadn't been inside this hospital in forty-five years—not since that week in early summer 1922, when he was born.

⚬🍃

One day after work, near the end of February 1969, Moshe Eshkenazi walked into the backyard of the house in Ramla, where Dalia was watering the flowers. He had the evening newspaper in his hands.

"Look what's in the papers," Moshe said to his daughter. "They've been investigating the Supersol bombing in Jerusalem. It says here that your friend Bashir is accused of taking part in this." He raised his eyebrows.

"Bashir Khairi of Ramallah?" Dalia asked. The article said that the bombing had been conducted by the Popular Front for the Liberation of Palestine, a group committed to "armed struggle," which the Israelis considered another name for terrorism.

Bashir in the PFLP? Dalia stood still, the watering can in her hands. She had opened her home to Bashir and his family, welcoming them whenever they came for a tour of the house and a visit to the garden and the lemon tree. In return she had received warmth and Arab hospitality. As the visits progressed, Dalia had learned more of the history of Bashir's family, and Bashir had begun to see that not every Israeli was the enemy. It had seemed to Dalia that a conversation based on common history and mutual interest was not so impossible.

The PFLP had recently commandeered several Israeli flights and held the passengers hostage. The group wanted to liberate Palestine, which to Dalia simply meant the destruction of Israel and the only home she knew.

The article said Bashir would be tried in an Israeli military court; maybe then the truth would come out. Dalia would attempt to withhold judgment until the trial. But already she was contemplating a disturbing question: Had she befriended a terrorist?

Bashir Khairi sat in a three-by-five-foot cell with stone walls, iron bars, and a low-watt bulb dangling from the ceiling. He slept on the concrete floor, and for six nights he lay in the dark, shivering without covers. He developed a high fever and chills. On the seventh day, his Israeli jailers brought him a blanket.

Bashir recalled being taken to an interrogation room, where a hood was placed over his head and he was beaten and choked. "Other times they would chain my hands and legs, blindfold me, and unleash the dogs. The dogs would jump on me and pin me against the wall. I could feel their breath on my neck."

After the interrogations came psychological operations. "In my cell," he said, "I would hear shots, and then someone screaming. Then the guards would arrive and bring me outside and show me a hole, and say, 'If you don't cooperate, this is where you'll end up.' Then I would be back in my cell, hearing shooting and screaming. You'd think: *They're killing the people who don't confess.*"

The Israeli interrogators wanted Bashir to admit to having played a role in the supermarket bombing and to describe the internal operations of the PFLP. Bashir admitted nothing. He refused to confirm any association with the PFLP. Consequently, the beatings, dog attacks, and psy-ops continued.

A week after Bashir went to prison, soldiers briefly brought him back to his house. They told his sister Nuha to come with them. She wasn't sure what they wanted, but got into a jeep with the soldiers and Bashir. He looked pale and weak.

"You look tired," Nuha said to her brother on the road to Jerusalem. "Did they beat you?"

"Stop!" the captain screamed at Nuha. "You can't talk to him!"

They arrived at a military investigation center. The soldiers brought Nuha into a small room and Bashir into the room next door. Shortly afterward, Nuha could hear Bashir's screams. After listening for what seemed like an interminable time, she couldn't bear to hear any more and fainted.

Three hours later, the jailers brought her a cup of water. They called her to the next room and opened the door. She saw Bashir, his head bowed, wearing only his underpants. Two men stood there, one on either side of him, wielding sticks.

"Brother," Nuha said. "Oh, my brother." The interrogators dragged Bashir away and told Nuha to find her own way back to Ramallah.

Bashir, by his own account, never admitted any connection to the supermarket bombing. "I endured the beatings, the hoods, and the dogs. They did not break me." He denied membership in the PFLP and disavowed any knowledge of its operations.

The *Sunday Times* of London eventually published a detailed investigation of the torture of Palestinian prisoners by Israel. The newspaper concluded, "Torture is organized so methodically that it cannot be dismissed as a handful of 'rogue cops' exceeding orders. It is systematic. It appears to be sanctioned at some level as deliberate policy."

The reasons for the torture, according to the *Sunday Times*, were threefold: to extract information; to "induce people to confess to 'security' offenses, of which, they may, or may not, be guilty," so officials could use those confessions to obtain convictions; and "to persuade Arabs in the occupied territories that it is least painful to behave passively. . . ." Israel denied the newspaper's allegations and defended their interrogations of suspected terrorists.

By now the world knew of the PFLP and the headline-grabbing operations that had terrorized Israelis. Many Palestinians had begun to realize that small guerrilla operations alone would not achieve their long-awaited liberation of Palestine. They came to embrace the PFLP's strategy of "spectacular operations" to reverse years of humiliation and failure and to focus the world's attention on the Palestinian plight.

From Cairo to Baghdad to Damascus to Amman, thousands of Arabs flooded rebel offices to volunteer in the renewed fight against

Israel. The "spectacular'" operations of the PFLP also began to attract legions of young Europeans, who saw in the airline hijackings a willingness to risk everything to achieve liberation. This was not just a time of cold war, but of revolution, inspired in part by massive and worldwide street protests against the Vietnam War. In some countries, the Vietcong were seen as freedom fighters and the United States as their oppressor. Similarly, the Palestinian rebels quickly became identified with the struggle for revolutionary justice against an occupying power.

The PFLP operations provoked a massive Israeli crackdown. Thousands of Palestinians were jailed and held indefinitely without charge. The PFLP tactics became a growing source of tension within the Palestinian nationalist movement. A new organization—the Democratic Front for the Liberation of Palestine—advocated for coexistence between Arabs and Jews within a single state, where no one would be forced to move, or for peaceful Arab and Jewish states existing side by side. Even among some of the radical factions of the Palestinian resistance, the idea of coexistence was gaining ground.

In 1970, PFLP fighters staged perhaps the most spectacular operation in the history of the Palestinian resistance. Their plan was to simultaneously hijack three New York–bound airliners from European capitals, thereby maximizing the number of U.S. passengers who would be affected and therefore also maximizing the amount of international attention they would get. The hijacked airliners would be forced to land in an old British airfield in the Jordanian desert, where the passengers would be held until Israel released Palestinian political prisoners.

PFLP operatives seized two of the flights and directed them to Jordan. The third attempt was foiled, but a few days later a Palestinian man single-handedly hijacked a British airliner and ordered the pilot to join the other two planes already on the ground in Jordan.

After six days, the crisis ended with all hostages safe and three charred jumbo jets in pieces on the tarmac, blown up by PFLP fighters (after the passengers were taken off the planes) to demonstrate their seriousness to the world.

The list of prisoners that the Palestinians had demanded be released in exchange for the Americans from the planes did not include Bashir. His name appeared on another prisoner-exchange list two years later, during a hijacking at the airport near Tel Aviv. That operation ended when Israeli commandos shot and killed the hijackers. Bashir remained in prison.

Chapter 17
CONVICTION

Dalia was sickened by the actions of the PFLP. Between classes at the university in Tel Aviv, or at home on the weekends, she wondered who these people were and how they thought they could achieve their goals with extreme and murderous tactics. She wondered about Bashir, too. Who was he, really?

Bashir was in jail: a member, according to Israeli authorities, of the PFLP. It was hard to believe that the same young man who had come to Dalia's door—whose family was received with such warmth in her home—could be part of the Popular Front. Dalia was stunned not because she had considered Bashir a friend, but because she had thought the connection was, in some ways, even deeper than that.

Through her encounters with the Khairis, Dalia, now twenty-one years old, had begun to question the stereotypes she was raised with: the stories of mistrust, suspicion, and hatred. "It was generally believed that an Arab can befriend you, but if their national interest dictates otherwise, they will stab you in the back with a knife," she said. "One had to fight against that, to prove that it's not true." Now, Dalia feared,

Bashir's perceptions of his own national interest had clashed completely with hers.

At the core of Dalia's faith was the conviction that personal dialogue was the key to transformation. If Bashir was in fact part of the PFLP, if he was connected to the Supersol bombing, it showed that "personal relationships meant nothing in the face of collective forces. If national interest comes before our common humanity," Dalia said, "then there is no hope for transformation, there is no hope for *anything*!"

One morning as preparations for Bashir's trial dragged on, Ahmad, Zakia, and Nuha decided to visit him in jail. Prison officials had moved him repeatedly, and now he sat in a cell in al-Ramla. Ahmad's eyesight was failing, but as they passed through the gates and into the visitors' area, he realized where he was. "Bashir," he said when his son arrived, "did you notice where this prison is? This is exactly where our olive trees used to be."

The land had remained in the family for at least twelve generations, until 1948. Bashir realized the symbolic was also the literal: he was imprisoned on his own land.

Soon, Ahmad decided he could no longer stay away from the house he'd built in 1936. He had always resisted, fearing he would not survive the shock of his return to the home he built. Now he and Zakia and Nuha stood at the door. Though Ahmad could barely see, he could make out the figure of a Jewish man in his mid-fifties: Moshe Eshkenazi. The two men stood facing each other across the threshold, two fathers of the same house.

They went through the house and outside again, to the garden in back. Ahmad walked slowly, touching the stones of the house. Moshe invited the guests to sit. Dalia and Solia were out on an errand.

Nuha recalled that Dalia arrived soon after and asked about Bashir. But three decades later Dalia had no such memories. She doesn't believe she ever met Ahmad, although she recalls her father telling her about the visit.

Before leaving, Ahmad said to Moshe, "There was a lemon tree here. I planted it. Is it still here?"

Nuha and Moshe led Ahmad to the tree. He extended his arms, running his fingers up the smooth, hard bark, over the soft knobs on the tree's base, and along the slender, narrowing branches until, between his hands, he felt the soft brush of leaves, and, between them, a small, cool sphere: a lemon from the tree he'd planted thirty-four years earlier. Zakia watched him in silence, tears in her eyes.

Ahmad was crying silently. Moshe plucked a few lemons and placed them in Ahmad's hands.

"Dalia's family—they were all very kind," Nuha recalled years later. "But what does that matter? They were the people who took our house."

In 1972, Bashir was sentenced to fifteen years in prison for complicity in the February 1969 bombing at the Supersol market and for membership in the outlawed PFLP. Israeli witnesses and Palestinian informants testified that Bashir had served as a liaison between the bomb makers and the PFLP members who hid the explosives at the market.

Bashir had expected the conviction. He stood and faced the judge. "I don't recognize this court," he said. "I'm innocent."

At no point did Bashir admit to any role in the bombing or to membership in the PFLP. "They could not extract a confession from me," he recalled more than twenty years later. "They were false accusations. Because if they had been able to prove it, I would have been sentenced to life in prison, not for fifteen years."

Bashir's co-defendants received harsher sentences. The convictions of some rested in part on the testimony of Israel Gefen, the veteran soldier who survived the blast.

After Bashir's conviction, Dalia immediately cut off all contact with the Khairi family. "I felt very betrayed," she recalled. Dalia had attached her deepest faith to the unfolding dialogue with Bashir. Now that was shattered, and along with it Dalia's belief in the power of "person-to-person relationships" to "touch the deeper humanity that goes beyond all national and political differences."

Bashir's commitment to his own cause, Dalia believed, meant that he was "determined that we should 'go back where we came from.' It meant that we were not wanted here." Alongside this anguish, there was a deep sense—more emotional than rational, Dalia would conclude later—that Bashir had confirmed a prejudice inherent to many Israelis: that Arabs kill Jews simply because they are Jews.

"Yeah, everything stopped," she recalled. "No contact. It was too much for me." The door she had opened was closed. Dalia became zealous in the defense of Israel and participated wholeheartedly in the nation's defense as an officer in the Israeli army.

When she got out of the service, Dalia plunged into her new work as an English teacher at the Ramla-Lod High School. The school was so close to the Ramla prison that the bricks of the two buildings actually touched.

Bashir spent the next twelve years in several Israeli prisons. His prison mates were other Palestinian men convicted of armed insurrection, of membership in banned political groups, or of demonstrating against the occupation. Some were simply waiting for formal charges to be filed against them. In the eighteen years following the Israeli occupation in June 1967, an estimated two hundred fifty thousand Palestinians—or 40 percent of the adult male population—had seen the inside of an Israeli jail.

Bashir lived the monotonous routine that defined prison life: up at 6:30, prison count, breakfast of one egg or a piece of bread and cheese, a morning of study, a lunch of thin soup, then an afternoon of more study, discussion, and rest. Exercise was discouraged, to prevent the prisoners from becoming physically stronger.

Prison study groups pored over works by Vladimir Lenin, Karl Marx, Pablo Neruda, Gabriel García Márquez, and other writers and revolutionaries. The men listened to Chopin, the great Arabic classical singer Umm Kulthum, and the Lebanese star Fayrouz as they played chess or backgammon on the floor of their cells. They gathered in a big circle to discuss the finer points of Soviet versus Chinese communism; political tensions in Vietnam, South Africa, Rhodesia, or Cuba; U.S. president Richard Nixon's and secretary of state Henry Kissinger's ventures in China and the Middle East; and the question of Palestine.

Bashir had become a committed Marxist and a leader among the prisoners. "He would always ask us to take something to other prisoners' families," said his sister Nuha. "Always he was helping the poor and needy families."

As the years passed, Nuha marked the events of her life that Bashir hadn't witnessed: her marriage to Ghiath, the cousin who had made the journey to al-Ramla with Bashir in 1967; the birth of her three sons; birthdays; anniversaries; celebrations.

For years, Dalia would walk past the Ramla prison on her way to work. Nearly every day, she thought about making contact with Bashir. At least, she thought, she could find out if he was there. Indeed, for a time he was. Yet she never inquired about him. Her urge to find out, she would say later, was outweighed by the desire not to know. *Why open a wound?* she thought. *Why start all this again?*

Dalia still felt "grievously betrayed." For years she had waited for some signal from Bashir, some indication that he was safe and that he was innocent, or sorry.

"If I am his friend, he can tell me *frankly*: 'I had nothing whatsoever to *do* with it,'" she said. "And yet he belongs to an organization that puts on its agenda to *destroy Israel*, also through *terror actions*— the so-called armed struggle. Bombing buses and so on where also Palestinians are. Where Palestinian *children* can be, because terror is indiscriminate. And *I* can be on one of these buses, too!

"I believed he was guilty," Dalia recalled. "I still believe so. And I would be the happiest person on earth to be disabused of this notion."

At her core, Dalia believed that what Bashir did, if he did it, "was not an answer. And if it was an answer, it is not an answer I can accept."

At times, Dalia would consider entering into a new discussion with the Khairi family. But then she would remember the Supersol bombing.

In the years Bashir spent in Israeli jails, wars would be fought and lost and leaders would rise and be shot down. An American president, Richard Nixon, resigned in disgrace, to be replaced by Gerald Ford, and then Jimmy Carter, who spoke of human rights and peace in the Middle East. Civil war broke out in Lebanon. In 1974 PLO leader Yasser Arafat addressed the United Nations in New York, to the fury of Israel and thousands of American demonstrators, but also to a standing ovation in the General Assembly, where he offered his dream of the "Palestine of tomorrow," in which Arab and Jew would live side by side in a secular, democratic state.

Bashir began to draw: first political caricatures, then map after map of Palestine, then more expressive renderings—uprooted trees, demolished houses, and Palestinians under arrest. As his Hebrew improved, he began to pressure Israeli prison officials for better meals and daily exercise for inmates. He organized hunger strikes to protest prison conditions. But he reported no changes.

In November 1977, Egyptian president Anwar Sadat, Israeli prime minister Menachem Begin, and U.S. president Jimmy Carter eventually signed an agreement—the Camp David Accords—that ended the state of war between Egypt and Israel.

For many in the West, in Israel, and in Egypt, Sadat was a hero. But many Palestinians, including Bashir, believed that the Egyptian president had sold them out by negotiating a deal that did not include a comprehensive settlement for all concerned. Demonstrations against Sadat and the Camp David Accords erupted across the occupied territories. Palestinians were still stateless, and the Israeli occupation was becoming even more entrenched. Now the Palestinians would need to go forward without Sadat. He even spawned a new word in the Palestinian Arab dialect: to this day, to be a *sadati* is to be one who is weak, one who capitulates, or one who acts cowardly.

In 1981, Sadat paid for his courage, or cowardice, with his life. He was assassinated by gunmen from Islamic Jihad in Cairo.

Throughout the 1970s, Dalia would often sit on her veranda in Ramla after work, gazing out at the Queen Elizabeth roses. She wondered if the conflict with the Palestinians would ever end. She knew that each side often seemed to wish the other away, but her own attempts to block the Khairi family from her mind were not working.

"Something within me kept pushing," she wrote years later. "A little nagging voice wished to figure out why it came to me to be involved in this. People came and knocked on my door, and I chose to open it. Is that door now forever shut?"

Dalia would recall hours of contemplation about the Khairi family and about the house she lived in, "which my father bought as 'abandoned property from the state.' But this house did not belong to the state; it belonged to the family that had built it, that had put its resources into it, that had hoped to raise its children and grow old in this house. I could imagine myself in the Khairis' place."

Is it either us or them? Dalia wondered. *Either I live in their house while they are refugees, or they live in my house while I become a fugitive? There must be another possibility. But what is it?*

Moshe and Solia were growing old. "I knew that one day," Dalia said, "I would inherit that house."

Chapter 18
SOLUTION?

In the fifteen years Bashir spent in one prison after another, he would from time to time talk about the young Israeli woman and the door she had opened for his family. "I told my friends in prison about my visits to the house," he recalled. "And what I saw in Dalia . . . I would say, 'She's open-minded, she's different compared with other Israelis that I met.' "

Yet Bashir would never write the letter Dalia so wanted. He did not confess to his Israeli interrogators, and he was not going to confess to Dalia. He maintained his innocence, though years later he said, "We have suffered many massacres. . . . In the face of these massacres and dispossessions, if anyone thought that the Palestinians would react as Jesus Christ would have, he is wrong. If I didn't have this deep conviction to the bone marrow in the necessity of hating the occupation, I wouldn't deserve to be a Palestinian."

Bashir was released from prison in September 1984. His family was waiting in Ramallah. Brothers and sisters returned from across the Arab world; they came from Amman, from Qatar, from Kuwait.

"It was like a wedding," Nuha recalled. "We prepared the best foods, sweets, flowers, Palestinian flags."

Many people heard that Bashir was to be released, and they gathered outside the prison to welcome him. When Israeli officials saw the crowd, they refused to let him out. His sister Khanom said the family waited from 8:00 a.m. until after 1:00 p.m.

When Bashir finally emerged, he went directly to the cemetery to pay respects to a co-defendant who had died in prison. "Then," Nuha said, "he came home."

So many people were waiting to see Bashir that friends had to direct traffic in front of the house. But Bashir did not like the idea of a celebration. "I am not a hero," he said. "I served my time—I did nothing special."

Adjusting to life outside of prison wasn't easy. "He slept on the floor, as he was not used to a bed anymore," Khanom said. His feet had changed from not wearing shoes, so he had trouble finding ones that weren't uncomfortable. Most disturbing were the marks of what his family believed was torture. "When he got out of prison, he had a lot of cigarette burns on his body," Khanom said. "When we asked him what they were, he said it was an allergy."

Three months after Bashir's release, Ahmad Khairi died. He was seventy-seven years old and had lived nearly half his life in exile. Later that year, Bashir married his cousin Scheherazade. In 1985, their first child was born. In the Arabic tradition, they named the boy after his grandfather, Ahmad.

Moshe Eshkenazi died that same year. Solia had died eight years earlier, and now no one lived in the house. "It was sad," Dalia remembered. "All your history is there, it's an empty house, your parents are dead." The house was legally hers, but "I could not deny that I lived in the house for all those years, while the family that built it had been expelled. How do you balance those realities? How do you confront them and respond to them?

"It was in my hands to do something," Dalia said. "It was like the house was telling me a story. More than one story. I had to respond."

Dalia always thought of the crime that had led to Bashir's long prison sentence. How could she respond in the light of that? Eventually she decided, "His reaction will not determine mine. I have free choice to think; I have free choice to act, in accordance with my understanding and my conscience."

Dalia had been thinking of the time when, as a little girl, she had wrenched the star and crescent, the symbol of Islam, from the top of the gate at the house in Ramla and thrown it away. "It was so beautiful," she said. "I wished I could put it back. I was ashamed of what I did."

One night, as she continued to mull over what to do about the house, the angel Gabriel came to her in a dream. "He was perched, hovering just there at the top of the gate where the crescent had been," Dalia said. "And he was looking at where the symbol was, and he was smiling. He was blessing the house, he was blessing me, and he was giving a blessing for what I wanted to do with the house."

A year after his release from prison, Bashir received a message from a Palestinian Anglican priest in Ramallah. The priest had been contacted by Yehezkel Landau, Dalia's husband, who explained that

Dalia wanted to meet with Bashir to talk about the future of the house.

Dalia knew that she wanted to act on the basis of two histories. "I had to acknowledge that this is my childhood home, my parents lived here until they died, my memories are all here, but that this house was built by another family, and their memories are here. I had to acknowledge absolutely all of it."

Within a month, Dalia and Yehezkel found themselves driving north into the occupied West Bank. They arrived at the home of the priest and his wife. Bashir was waiting there.

Dalia and Bashir sat facing each other in comfortable chairs in the living room. How long had it been? Sixteen years? Eighteen? Dalia was now thirty-seven, with a wedding ring on her finger, and Bashir, forty-three, was also newly married. A tuft of gray hair fell over his forehead. Dalia noticed that his left hand was in his pocket, as it always seemed to be.

They exchanged small talk. Was Bashir healthy? What were his plans?

Dalia came to the point of the meeting. She had been thinking about the cycle of pain, retaliation, pain, retaliation. She wondered if there was something she could do to address that and to honor the families' two histories. This was not just a gesture to Bashir, but to the entire Khairi family. *How does one acknowledge the collective wound?* she had asked herself again and again. *The heart wants to move toward the healing of that wound.*

Dalia understood that she couldn't share ownership of the house with the Khairis, or even transfer the title to their name. Another solution was needed. Dalia raised the possibility that she could sell the house and give the proceeds to the Khairis.

"No, no, no," Bashir said quickly. "No selling. Our patrimony cannot be for sale."

"Then how do you see it, Bashir?" Dalia asked. "What shall we do?"

For Bashir, the solution had to be consistent with his rights and his lifelong struggle as a Palestinian. "This house is my homeland," he said. "I lost my childhood there. I would like the house to provide a very nice time for the Arab children of al-Ramla. I want them to have joy there. I want them to have the childhood that I never had. What I lost there, I want to give to them."

Dalia and Yehezkel agreed readily to Bashir's suggestion: the house would become a school for young Arab children of Israel.

The conversation continued as the group sat down for dinner. As they prepared to break bread, Dalia and Yehezkel looked across the table at their Arab neighbors and offered a prayer in Hebrew:

Blessed are You, the eternal One,
Our God, Ruler of the universe,
Who brings forth bread from the earth.

Chapter 19
DALIA'S LETTER

Bashir lay blindfolded and facedown in an Israeli military van rolling south from the West Bank town of Nablus. His hands were cuffed behind him, his legs shackled and attached by chains to three other prisoners.

His freedom hadn't lasted. Three years after his release from prison, Bashir Khairi was in custody again. That morning—January 13, 1988—Bashir and three other men had been taken from their cells at Jneid prison in Nablus and led along the concrete floor toward the prison exit. The action would come as no surprise to the international diplomatic community, the press, human rights lawyers, the Arab world, and the eight hundred Palestinians behind bars at Jneid. The arrest of the four men was part of a broader Israeli crackdown on the suspected organizers of the ongoing disturbances in Gaza and the West Bank, known to Israelis as riots and to the Arab world as the uprising—in Arabic, the intifada.

Five weeks earlier, on December 8, 1987, an Israeli vehicle veered into a long line of cars carrying Palestinian men returning to Gaza from low-paying day labor in Israel. Four Arabs were killed. Rumors spread that the corpses of the four men had been seized from the Jabalya refugee camp by Israeli troops attempting to cover up evidence that the men had been murdered.

As several thousand people gathered in the camp for the funeral, clashes broke out. The next day, boys and young men began hurling stones at Israeli soldiers. The troops responded with live fire, and a young man was killed.

The demonstrations spread quickly, first to Gaza and then to the West Bank, as young men, teenagers, and even boys as young as eight threw stones at Israeli soldiers and tanks. The intifada was born.

Now the image of Palestinians that splashed across the world's television screens was not of hijackers but of young people throwing stones at occupiers who responded with bullets. Israel, long portrayed in the West as David in a hostile Arab sea, was suddenly cast as Goliath.

For years, the PLO, a coalition of nationalist resistance groups with Yasser Arafat's Fatah at its center, had dominated Palestinian politics. Five days into the intifada, however, a new group emerged from the same Gaza refugee camp that had spawned the uprising. It would be called the Islamic Resistance Movement, known by its Arabic acronym, Hamas.

Hamas favored no recognition of Israel and no compromise on the right of return, and sought an Islamic state in all of historic Palestine. But resistance in the intifada went far beyond Hamas. Much of it was spontaneous, with local committees backing hit-and-run operations against Israeli platoons; conducting secret classes when Israeli authorities closed schools; and forming bread, poultry, and sewing cooperatives to replace income when the men could no longer work in Israel.

At least two hundred thirty Palestinians were killed by Israeli troops in the first year of the uprising, and more than twenty thousand were arrested. Israeli officials closed nine hundred West Bank and Gaza schools, imposed broad curfews that prevented workers from getting to their jobs, and began to deport to Lebanon the men—including Bashir—who were suspected of organizing the intifada.

Bashir and three other men were described in an Israeli military court as "among the leaders and instigators" of the disturbances. The judge approved their deportations, despite objections from many nations, including the United States, and a strongly worded resolution from the United Nations Security Council.

The men were blindfolded and pushed into a helicopter, which crossed Israel's northern border and set down on a road in southern Lebanon.

Bashir stepped beneath the helicopter blades and felt someone take off his blindfold. An officer gave him fifty dollars and looked him in the eye. "If you even try to come back," he said, "we will shoot you."

"ISRAEL DEFIES UN AND DEPORTS FOUR PALESTINIANS" read a headline in the January 14 edition of the *Times* of London. That same day, the *Jerusalem Post* reported that Bashir and the other three men had been "shuttled secretly by helicopter to the northern edge of the Southern Lebanon Security Zone at noon yesterday, without a word of notice to their families or lawyers." The deportations were widely denounced around the world as a human rights violation and counterproductive to any peaceful solution to the conflict.

In that same January 14 edition of the *Jerusalem Post*, at the back of the paper on the editorial page, a quiet voice emerged amid the international furor. The voice belonged to a forty-year-old woman who had grown up in Ramla. Her essay was titled "Letter to a Deportee."

"Dear Bashir," Dalia wrote. "We got to know each other twenty years ago under unusual and unexpected circumstances. Ever since we have become part of each other's lives. Now I hear that you are about to be deported. Since you are in detention at present, and this may be my last chance to communicate with you, I have chosen to write this open letter. First, I want to retell our story."

Dalia was writing from a hospital bed in Jerusalem. Nine months earlier, she'd been diagnosed with cancer. Doctors recommended treatment that would include a hysterectomy. She agreed to the procedure, but just days before the surgery Dalia discovered that she was pregnant. Against the advice of her doctors, she refused the surgery, putting her life at risk. She was soon confined to a hospital bed for twenty-four hours a day.

When her husband told Dalia that Bashir was being deported, he also suggested that she write about her history with Bashir. She dismissed the suggestion at first, but then "an inner voice, an inner conviction" rose up in her, "welling up in a wave, saying, *Yes, it's right to do it. You've got to do it.*"

Dalia recounted for Israeli readers the story of the Eshkenazis, the Khairis, and the house in Ramla. She told of Bashir's first visit to her after the Six-Day War, of her visit to Ramallah, and of the "warm personal connection" they'd established across the gulf of political differences and her understanding that the house she grew up in was not simply "abandoned property":

> *It was very painful for me, as a young woman 20 years ago, to wake up to a few then well hidden facts. For example, we were all led to believe the Arab population of Ramla and Lod had run away before the advancing Israeli army in 1948, leaving everything*

behind in a rushed and cowardly escape. This belief reassured us. It
was meant to prevent guilt and remorse. But after 1967, I met not
only you, but also an Israeli Jew who had personally participated in
the expulsion from Ramla and Lod. He told me the story as he had
experienced it, and as Yitzhak Rabin (who would later become
Israel's prime minister) later confirmed in his memoirs.

My love for my country was losing its innocence . . . some
change in perspective was beginning to take place in me.

She recounted the day of Ahmad Khairi's only visit to the house
and the moment when he stood at the lemon tree, tears rolling
down his face, as Moshe Eshkenazi placed a few lemons in Ahmad's
hands:

> *Many years later, after the death of your father, your mother*
> *told me that, whenever he felt troubled at night and could not*
> *sleep, he would pace up and down your rented apartment in*
> *Ramallah, holding a shriveled lemon in his hand. It was the same*
> *lemon my father had given him on that visit.*
>
> *Ever since I met you, the feeling has been growing in me that*
> *that home was not just my home. The lemon tree which yielded so*
> *much fruit and gave us so much delight lived in other people's*
> *hearts too. The spacious house with its high ceilings, big windows*
> *and large grounds was no longer just an "Arab house," a desirable*
> *form of architecture. It had faces behind it now. The walls evoked*
> *other people's memories and tears.*

Dalia described a "strange destiny" that connected her family to
Bashir's. Though the plans for turning the house into a school and

center for Arab-Jewish dialogue had been long delayed, this "destiny" was still on her mind: "The house with which our childhood memories were connected forces us to face each other." But now she wondered whether reconciliation could be possible across a chasm as wide as the one between herself and Bashir. She wrote of Bashir's conviction and prison term in the aftermath of the explosion that had killed three civilians in the Supersol market, and then pleaded with Bashir to transform his politics:

> *People like yourself, Bashir, bear a great responsibility for triggering our anxieties which are well justified, given the PFLP's determination to replace Israel with a "secular democratic state" and to use terror to achieve this aim.*
>
> *If you could disassociate yourself from your past terrorist actions, your commitment to your own people would gain true moral force in my eyes. I well understand that terror is a term relative to a subjective point of view. Some of Israel's political leaders were terrorists in the past and have never repented. I know that what we consider terror from our side, your people consider their heroic "armed struggle" with the means at their disposal. What we consider our right to self-defense, when we bomb Palestinian targets from the air and inevitably hit civilians, you consider mass terror from the air with advanced technology. Each side has an ingenuity for justifying its own position.*

Dalia then turned to the actions of her own government in deporting Bashir, which she called a "violation of human rights" that created more bitterness and extremism among Palestinians:

You, Bashir, have already experienced one expulsion from Ramla as a child. Now you are about to experience another from Ramallah forty years later. You will thus become a refugee twice. You may be separated from your wife and your two small children, Ahmad and Hanine, and from your elderly mother and the rest of your family. How can your children avoid hating those who will have deprived them of their father? Will the legacy of pain grow and harden with bitterness as it passes down from generations?

It seems to me, Bashir, that you will now have a new opportunity to assume a leadership role. By its intention to deport you, Israel is actually empowering you. I appeal to you to demonstrate the kind of leadership that uses nonviolent means of struggle for your rights . . .

I appeal to both Palestinians and Israelis to understand that the use of force will not resolve this conflict on its fundamental level. This is the kind of war that no one can win, and either both peoples will achieve liberation or neither will.

Our childhood memories, yours and mine, are intertwined in a tragic way. If we can not find means to transform that tragedy into a shared blessing, our clinging to the past will destroy our future. We will then rob another generation of a joy-filled childhood and turn them into martyrs for an unholy cause. I pray that with your cooperation and God's help, our children will delight in the beauty and bounties of this holy land.

Allah ma'ak. May God be with you.

Dalia

Bashir did not read Dalia's open letter for weeks. The morning it appeared in print, he and the three other deportees were well inside

Lebanese territory at a PFLP training camp. Like the Palestinians in refugee camps across Lebanon, they were stateless, unwanted by the Lebanese authorities and determined to return home. But unlike the refugees, their deportations had drawn international attention, which they intended to exploit to the full advantage of the Palestinian cause, and to the intifada in particular.

Their idea was to set up tents as close as possible to the southernmost border of Lebanon, with Israel just beyond. By hiding in the back of an ambulance, they made their way to an office of the International Red Cross. They knew that the Red Cross would not be pleased to see them, but neither would the organization be in a position to expel them.

Bashir and the others pitched a tent and a Palestinian flag in front of the Red Cross office. Within hours, local supporters arrived with more tents. Soon the four men were at the center of a widening group of activists, dignitaries, and the international press. "I can't remember a night where there weren't at least one hundred people," Bashir would say.

PLO and PFLP leaders came to see them. Officials throughout the Arab world discussed their status.

For some Palestinians, the solution was Israel's withdrawal to its 1967 border and the creation of a Palestinian state on the other side of the line. But for Bashir and hundreds of thousands of refugees, that compromise would not go far enough. They believed in the earlier UN resolution, which endorsed their right to go back to their homes in what was now Israel.

"The only solution is return," Bashir told reporters as he stood among the tents in the Red Cross field. "We want to go back to our homeland."

Chapter 20
BASHIR'S REPLY

In May 1988, Nuha and Ghiath Khairi visited Dalia's hospital room in Jerusalem. They had heard from Bashir.

As they walked into the room, Dalia's eyes were drawn to Nuha, elegant and dignified, with her reddish-brown hair done perfectly. For the last four months, ever since Dalia's letter had been published, Dalia had received a steady stream of visitors, including many reporters and television producers. "Sometimes it got to be too much for me," she remembered, but when Nuha and Ghiath arrived, "I felt an affinity."

"We have been waiting to visit for a long time," Ghiath said. They asked about Dalia's health and the baby, and Dalia replied that she was scheduled to have a cesarean section in two days.

Ghiath told Dalia that Bashir had written a response to her open letter, and that a journalist, serving as a messenger, would deliver it soon.

"How is Ahmad?" Dalia asked, referring to Bashir and Scheherazade's boy, who was now three. Hanine, their daughter, was still a baby.

"He is asking for his father," Nuha said.

"What do you tell him?"

"That the Jews have deported him."

Dalia imagined what was going through the boy's mind. *Young Ahmad lives with a great enemy, the Jews. The evil that has the power to take his father away from him.*

Ghiath spoke up. "In 1967, I went to my father's house. I remember when my father built it. Tell me," he said, looking at Yehezkel, "why, why did your people come to our country?"

Yehezkel started to speak, but Ghiath continued: "Why should it be at my expense?"

"We too felt in exile for all these years," Yehezkel replied. "Don't you feel in exile?"

"Yes, I do," Ghiath said. "I would rather sleep under a lamppost in al-Ramla than in a palace in Ramallah."

"Your children were not born in Ramla. Don't they feel the same?"

"Yes, they do feel the same."

"And their children, will they not feel the same?"

"Yes, indeed they will."

"So have we," said Yehezkel. "Our forefathers and the fathers of our forefathers."

Dalia, flat on her back in the hospital bed, was struck that Ghiath could not understand her people's longing for the ancient homeland.

"But they were not born here," Ghiath protested. "For example, my Jewish friend, Avraham, he and his father and his forefathers were born here. Their family is from Jaffa. He is a true Palestinian."

So that means, Dalia thought, *that I'm not?*

"It's a different kind of self-understanding," countered Yehezkel, the religious scholar. "Why do you think Israelis are afraid of you?

We are not as afraid of the entire Syrian army with all its weaponry as we are of you. Why do you think that is?"

Ghiath looked at Yehezkel in amazement as Yehezkel continued: "Because you are the only ones who have a legitimate grievance against us. And deep down, even those who deny it know it. That makes us very uncomfortable and uneasy in dealing with you. Because our homes are your homes, you become a real threat."

"Why can't we all live in the same state, together in peace?" Ghiath asked. "Why do we need two states?"

"Then you think you would be able to go back to your father's house?" Yehezkel replied.

Dalia shifted in her bed. "And what would happen to the people already living in those houses?" she asked.

"They will build new homes for them," Ghiath said.

"You mean," Dalia said, "they will be evacuated for you to return to your original houses? I hope you can understand why Israelis are afraid of you. Israel will do everything to prevent the implementation of these dreams. Even under a peace plan you will not return to your original homes."

The back-and-forth continued. "Why do you need a state of your own?" Ghiath asked. "And if you do need one, why could you not have gone to Uganda, or to another place, many years ago? How many Arabs are there now in the USA? Do they demand a state of their own in the USA?"

Dalia said, "I'm not going to explain to you what the yearning for Zion means to us. I will just say that because you see us as strangers in this land, that is why we are afraid of you. . . . The Palestinian people as a collective have not accepted the Jewish home in this land. Most of you still consider us a cancerous presence among you. I struggle for your rights despite my fears. But your rights have to be balanced against our needs for survival. . . . In a peace plan, *everybody will have to do with less than they deserve.*"

No one spoke for a few minutes. It was getting late, and Nuha and Ghiath had to get back to Ramallah.

Ghiath said to Yehezkel, "May you have a son!"

Nuha looked at Dalia and said, "They only dream of sons. Everyone."

Ghiath continued, "And may he think like you, Yehezkel."

"I am a Jew and a Zionist," Yehezkel replied, "and if he thinks like me, he will be a Jew and a Zionist!"

By now everyone was laughing. Ghiath said, to more laughter, "I will give him Islamic books to read, and you never know what your son will think!"

As they prepared to leave, Nuha leaned close to Dalia and took her hand. "May you bear a healthy child," she said. "*Ehsh'Allah.*" God willing.

Two days later, Raphael Ya'acov Avichai Landau was born by c-section. His name—Raphael—meant "God's healing." Dalia had spent months in a hospital bed, hooked to intravenous drips and beeping machines. Now she held her healthy baby boy in her arms.

In late 1988, Yasser Arafat announced his unconditional support for the UN resolution that included Israel's right "to live in peace within secure and recognized boundaries free from threats or acts of force." He also renounced "all forms of terrorism."

Bashir was not happy. If the Palestinians accepted the resolution, they would have to accept Israel's right to exist. And if they accepted

Israel and the "solution" of two states, what would happen to Bashir's right of return to al-Ramla, which was in the state of Israel? Bashir felt that he had not spent more than half of his adult life in prison, enduring humiliation, torture, statelessness, and now deportation, for a compromise like the one Arafat seemed to be considering.

Bashir was not alone. The following summer, Fatah, the mainstream PLO faction that had been founded by Arafat, endorsed renewed armed struggle against Israel.

Bashir had read Dalia's open letter many times. He was moved by her public acknowledgment of the expulsions from al-Ramla and Lydda (Lod) and her other declarations. But he was also struck by Dalia's references to his "past terrorist actions" and her admonishment that he transform his politics and embrace nonviolence.

For months, Bashir had been thinking of the best way to respond to Dalia. He had something important to tell her, something that in the twenty-one years he had known her, he had never revealed.

"Dear Dalia," his letter began.

> It's true that we got acquainted as you mentioned in your letter in exceptional and unexpected circumstances. . . . And it's true that after we got acquainted, each one of us has become part of the life of the other. I don't deny that what I've sensed in you, Dalia, of morality, sensitivity and sensibility, left a deep impact in me that I cannot ignore.

The letter was typed on single-spaced pages and was stuffed into a thick envelope. It continued:

*Your letter came in the period of my exile from my land, from
the land of my country, Palestine, after our dialogue, conversations
and acquaintance had become the talk of the press in the media,
and even the talk of all the people whose consciousness was moved
to recognize the truth of what's really happening and to reassess
what happened.*

*Allow me first to express my affection and respect as well as
appreciation of your courage to write to me, and your courage
to present the ideas contained in your letter. Please allow me to
present my respect to your husband Yehezkel Landau, who I have
a lot of appreciation for . . .*

Bashir's letter, Dalia saw, reflected the many hours of conversation the two had had before Bashir went to prison in 1969: tremendous personal warmth that somehow bridged a chasm of anguish and
mistrust. Now she read as he countered her suggestion that any
of his actions had "planted hatred." Instead, he wrote, "the Zionist
leadership has planted hatred in the souls of one generation after
another."

*[It] destroyed all human values the day it destroyed our
childhood, our existence, and our right to live on the soil of
our homeland. Your change, Dalia, and your new perspective was
attained through research and investigation. And your ability to
see things the way they are in reality, not the way they were told
to you.*

*We were exiled by the force of arms. We were exiled on foot.
We were exiled to take the earth as our bed. And the sky as a
cover. . . . We were exiled but we left our souls, our hopes and our*

childhood in Palestine. We left our joys and sorrow. We left them in every corner, and on every grain of sand in Palestine. We left them with each lemon fruit, with each olive. We left them in the roses and flowers. We left them in the flowering tree that stands with pride at the entrance of our house in al-Ramla. We left them in the remains of our fathers and ancestors. We left them as witnesses and history. We left them, hoping to return.

Bashir then revealed the secret he'd kept from Dalia all those years. The family was in Gaza, late in 1948, shortly after arriving from Ramallah. Six-year-old Bashir and his siblings had been playing in the dirt yard outside their cinder block house. They saw something gleaming in the sun. It was bulbous, with a wick protruding. It looked like a lantern. The children brought it inside, and Bashir held the new toy as the other children gathered around. One of the children bumped into a clay water jug, and it crashed to the floor. The other children scattered. Bashir was left alone with the toy. Suddenly it exploded.

"The booby-trapped toy exploded in my left hand to crush my palm, to scatter my bones and flesh," Bashir wrote. "And shed my blood, to blend it with the soil of Palestine. To embrace the lemon fruits and the olive trees, to cling to the dates and the flowers of the fitna tree."

Bashir lost four fingers and the palm of his left hand.

Who is more entitled to a reunion, Dalia? Sharansky, the Russian who doesn't have a cultural linguistic historic attachment to Palestine? Or the Palestinian Bashir, who is attached to Palestine with the language, culture, history, family and the remains of my palm that I left in Palestine? Does not the world owe

me the right to reunite myself, to reunite my palm with my body?
Why do I have to live without my identity and without my
homeland while my palm remains in Palestine?

Dalia stared at the page in amazement. How could she have known Bashir for so long and not known he was missing his left hand? Slowly it came to her: his hand was always in his pocket. She had only ever seen the left thumb, hitched over the top of his pocket. It looked so natural.

Dalia realized that for nearly all of his life, Bashir had blamed the Zionists for placing booby-trapped "toys" in the sands of Gaza in order to maim Palestinian children. "I was amazed at the intensity of his perception that Zionism was this incredibly evil manifestation and that this was his experience," she said. "There was no way I could accept this description of the Zionists, my people, me, as being the expression of darkness. To me Zion is an expression of my very ancient longing, for me it's a word that symbolizes a harbor for my people and our collective expression here. And for him, it's a regime of terror. Something that's an obligation to fight. And to resist in every way. Because for him if Zionism is a reign of terror, then terrorism is an appropriate answer!"

Dalia paused and gathered herself. "And I say that I cannot afford to fight one wrong with another wrong. It doesn't lead *anywhere!*"

Bashir had neared the end of his letter. "I don't want to overburden you, Dalia," he wrote.

I know how sensitive you are. I know how you hurt. I don't wish
you any pain. All that I wish is for you and me to struggle together
with all of the peace and freedom loving people for the

establishment of a democratic popular state. And to struggle to
bring the idea of the Dalia child care center to life. And to struggle
with me for my return to my old mother, to my wife and my
children, to my homeland, to struggle with me to reunite with
my palm, my palm that has blended with every grain of Palestinian
soil.

> *Yours with respect, faithfully,*
> *Bashir*

Dalia sat quietly for a long time, "quite shaken," gazing at the letter. She had long heard Bashir's proposal that the land of Israel and Palestine be transformed into a single democratic secular state for all the people of historic Palestine. She believed, however, that a single state meant the end of Israel, and for this reason she could not endorse Bashir's idea. It was true that Dalia had offered to return her house to Bashir, or at least to find some way to share its legacy, but she would go to great lengths to explain that this was a personal choice, not to be understood as an endorsement of a broader right of return.

It seemed inevitable that Bashir and Dalia would never reconcile their differences.

Chapter 21
OPEN HOUSE

Shortly after she received Bashir's letter, Dalia drove from her home in Jerusalem to her hometown of Ramla. It was time to honor the common history of the Khairi and Eshkenazi families. She drove past Ramla City Hall—an Arab house that once belonged to Sheikh Mustafa Khairi—and parked outside the office of the city's cultural center. She soon found herself shaking hands with a young Arab man named Michail Fanous.

The Fanous family history in Ramla went back centuries. Michail's father, Salem, a Christian minister, had been held as a prisoner of war by the Israeli army after the occupation of 1948.

Michail had spent much of his thirty years trying to reconcile his identity as a Christian Palestinian citizen of Israel. When his classmates insisted other Arabs had fled Ramla like cowards, Michail would shout, "*No*, they didn't, just ask my father!"

By 1989, Michail had been elected to the Ramla City Council—only the second Arab since 1948. He advocated for the rights of the Arab minority in Israel, which made up nearly 20 percent of the population.

Dalia told Michail her story and the story of the house, which had been the center of her life and Bashir's. Both Michail and Dalia wanted to do something for the Arab population and provide a place where Arabs and Jews could meet. Dalia proposed that Michail be the Christian Arab partner in an enterprise that would give witness to the history of Arabs and Jews. It would include a school for the Arab children of Ramla and a center for Arab-Jewish coexistence.

In October 1991, the first four Arab kindergarten children walked through the doors that Ahmad Khairi had framed and secured fifty-five years earlier. This was the beginning of Bashir's dream: to bring joy to the Arab children of al-Ramla. Soon the mission would expand, incorporating the vision of Dalia, Yehezkel, and Michail: to be a place of encounter between Arabs and Jews.

They would call it Open House.

Bashir sat in the shade near the eastern end of the Allenby Bridge, which connected the kingdom of Jordan with Palestine, the land of his birth. It was April 1996, a warm spring morning in the Jordan Valley. Bashir, now 54 years old, rested on a bench outside the Jordanian passport control building, waiting to cross. Finally a bus arrived. Bashir and the other passengers climbed on and rode past military sentry posts and through a series of checkpoints and razor wire fences. The bus crossed the bridge over the narrow trickle of the once great Jordan River—diminished by upstream dams and diversions to a weed-lined ditch separating Hussein's kingdom from the Israeli-occupied West Bank. Anyone foolish enough to jump from the East Bank to the West would be more likely to get shot than wet.

After years of secret negotiations, a peace agreement between

Israeli and Palestinian leaders had paved the way for Bashir to come back to Palestine. But his return was bittersweet. Eight years after being deported by Israeli authorities, Bashir would soon be reunited with his wife and children in Ramallah. But like hundreds of other returning Palestinians, Bashir had dreamed of a different kind of return—all the way back to the homes they had lost in 1948. Instead, Palestinian leaders had agreed to a partial return, only to the West Bank and Gaza. Bashir felt betrayed.

The bus rolled slowly toward Israeli military security in the occupied West Bank. A guard pulled Bashir aside. For several hours, he was interrogated. Finally, he was released, and walked through the security gates and into the open air of the West Bank, and the arms of his family.

For many Palestinians and Israelis alike, there were plenty of encouraging signs. At Open House, now in its fifth year in the house in Ramla, Dalia and Yehezkel had seen more willingness among Israelis to engage in Arab-Jewish dialogue. Summer peace camps with Arab and Jewish children were popular, and Yehezkel believed "the whole coexistence approach was legitimized in the eyes of Jews."

Dalia remembered how she had concluded her letter to Bashir seven years earlier: "I pray that with your cooperation and God's help, our children will delight in the beauty and bounties of this holy land."

On November 4, 1995, Dalia thought these dreams were still possible. That evening, Israeli prime minister Yitzhak Rabin addressed a crowd of one hundred thousand at a square in Tel Aviv. The people had gathered in support of peace with the Palestinians. Rabin, who had fought against the Arabs in 1948, 1956, and 1967; who had authorized "might, force, and beatings" against Palestinian youths in the intifada; and who for years had opposed recognition of the PLO, told the crowd that "I believe there is now a chance for peace, a great chance, which must be seized." He said that the gathering was "proof that the nation truly wants peace and rejects violence. Violence is undermining the foundations of Israeli democracy. It must be rejected and condemned, and it must be contained. It is not the way of the state of Israel."

The crowd began to sing "Shir l'Shalom," a song from the perspective of the sorrowful voices of the dead, speaking to the living. It had become the anthem of the Israeli peace movement. Rabin sang along.

As the rally ended, Rabin left the podium and headed toward his motorcade.

At about that same moment, Dalia was riding in a taxi in Jerusalem. At a stoplight the cab encountered another taxi driver, who shouted through his window, "Rabin has been shot!"

Dalia couldn't digest the words. *This isn't possible*, she thought. *It can't be.*

"Oh, my goodness," the driver told Dalia in Hebrew. "I have no radio!" He sped toward West Jerusalem. At each light they signaled to other cars and asked, "What happened?"

Rabin was dead, shot at point-blank range by a twenty-year-old religious law student.

Dalia stayed up until morning, watching television, completely bewildered. "There was an immense sense that something was lost," she recalled. "This was a man who had gone through tremendous change. . . . Who could have thought that terror would hit home in such a way?"

Dalia and Yehezkel wondered if Rabin and Arafat could have worked together to actually bring peace. Dalia had her doubts about whether Rabin "could have brought his entire people along with him. But I felt terribly hurt. I felt that good people that could make a difference—they don't stand a chance."

The toxic atmosphere continued, and came to a head for Dalia and Yehezkel in 2002, when a suicide bomber detonated a bomb on a bus near their home. Their son, Raphael, was on a bus to school when they received a phone call alerting them of the bombing. Raphael's bus had just passed through that neighborhood.

Yehezkel rushed to turn on the television, where he learned that the explosion had occurred on a municipal bus, not Raphael's school bus. But some children had been killed on the municipal bus.

The bus had exploded during the Jewish celebration of Chanukah, which is marked by the lighting of candles on eight consecutive nights. In the coming days, Dalia and Yehezkel made regular trips to the bus stop where the bombing had occurred. Residents and visitors had erected a shrine of candles, wreaths, newspaper clippings, photos of the dead, prayer books, and other items. Alongside the expressions of grief were signs promising to avenge the killings: "No Arabs, No Terror." "The way to true peace: If someone comes to kill you, thwart him by killing him first!"

Dalia watched as families left Israel, seeking safe haven in Europe, the United States, or Australia. "Many people are leaving Israel to find a place of safety elsewhere, to protect their children," she wrote in her journal in the late fall of 2002. "But isn't that what our enemies want? Yet, on the other hand, Raphael too could have been on that bus. What is the responsible thing to do under the circumstances? There are many people in Israel who have no family or friends in other parts of the world. They do not have the luxury of the choices that I have here. Am I going to abandon them? My choice is to stay here."

Chapter 22
HEART

Dalia sat in the passenger seat of a rental car, staring straight ahead and trying to look casual, as if she, too, were a journalist and as if it was normal for her to cross the Israeli military checkpoint heading north from Jerusalem to Ramallah. In fact, it was forbidden for Israeli civilians to travel to the occupied territories, and Dalia knew she risked being turned back. The soldier, however, checked only the driver's American passport, and surprisingly, the gamble paid off: Dalia was through the checkpoint and on her way to Ramallah.

"Oh, my god," Dalia gasped. A long line of vehicles pointed south, nearly frozen in place. Young Palestinian men and boys passed between the cars, offering gum, cactus fruit, cucumbers, kitchen utensils, and soap for sale to the frustrated, immobile drivers.

Just behind the cars and the hawkers stood the subject of Dalia's exclamation: a towering curtain of concrete, stretching out of sight to the north. This was Israel's "security barrier," separating the West Bank from Israel and, in some cases, the West Bank from itself. Construction of the barrier had begun in 2002 and included six thousand workers digging trenches, stringing razor wire, erecting guard posts, laying concrete, and installing tens of thousands of electronic sensors.

"The sole purpose of the fence," Israel declared, "is to provide security" in response to "the horrific wave of terrorism emanating from the West Bank."

The rental car bumped along potholed roads, passed under a banner welcoming visitors to Ramallah, and stopped near a shop. Bashir stood waiting at the second-floor landing.

Bashir and Dalia stood in the hallway outside his office and shook hands for a long time, smiling broadly. "*Keef hallek*?" Bashir asked. "How are you, Dalia?"

Dalia handed Bashir a white paper bag with green lettering in Hebrew. "A little lemon cake, Bashir," she said.

Bashir led Dalia into his office and asked about Yehezkel and Raphael.

"Raphael is sixteen now. He's in high school. He likes computers. And I hear Ahmad is eighteen and going to Harvard!"

"It's only for four years. Now I am getting old. I'm sixty-two."

"The gray looks good!" Dalia said, beaming at Bashir. "Wonderful!"

Bashir had been smiling from the moment Dalia arrived; now his face changed. "I'm eager to see you, but I was afraid for you. Especially with the news of each day. The wall, the arrests, the house demolitions, the way it is. The situation is not quiet. You can see people tense. You never know what could happen."

Dalia wanted to know if Bashir had been in prison in Ramla when she was teaching high school next door in 1971.

"Maybe I was there, in solitary confinement," Bashir replied. "I was there less than one year. I was in seventeen prisons."

Bashir spoke about meeting with Yitzhak Rabin while Bashir was in one of the prisons. He exhorted Rabin to do something to improve conditions for the prisoners.

"It's interesting that he would come as minister of defense to sit with the prisoners," Dalia said.

"I was a prisoner. He was minister of defense. Nothing changed."

"But Bashir," Dalia said, "don't you think that someone like that, who did something to change—made some progress, as much as he could in changing his position, to move a little bit—to make a compromise and extend his hand to your people . . . ?" Her question was left unfinished.

Bashir leaned forward. "For Palestinians it didn't change the daily life. It went from bad to worse. I didn't go back to al-Ramla. We don't have our independent state, and we don't have our freedom. . . . I can't even be on the board of the Open House because I'm Palestinian, not Israeli. If somebody comes yesterday from Ethiopia but he's Jewish, he will have all the rights, when I'm the one who has the history in al-Ramla. But for them I'm a stranger."

Dalia's arms were folded tightly across her chest. She unfolded them and took a breath.

"Bashir," she said. "Maybe I have no right to say what I'm going to say. We need to make sacrifices if both of us are to live here. *We need to make sacrifices.* And I know it is not fair for me to say that. I know. I mean, you cannot live in your house in Ramla. I know it's not fair. But I think we do need to strengthen those people who are willing to make some compromise. Like Rabin, who paid with his life. And so for your country, you need to strengthen the hand of those who are ready to make a compromise and ready to make space for us here. By not accepting the state of Israel or by not accepting the state of Palestine, I think none of us has a real life here."

Dalia took another long breath and continued. "If I knew or if we knew that you could make space for the state of Israel, first of all in your heart, then we could find a solution on the ground. How much less threatened my people would feel. I say this understanding that I don't even have a right to ask you for this. I'm just asking this. That is my plea."

Bashir spoke of their first meeting, thirty-seven years before, when he visited the house in al-Ramla. "And since then there have been more settlements, land confiscations, and now this wall—how can there be any solution? How can there be any Palestinian state? How can I open my heart, as you say?" He continued to believe that without return, the conflict would be eternal.

"We are weak today," Bashir said. "But we won't stay this way. Palestinians are stones in the riverbed. We won't be washed away."

Dalia's chin rested in her palm, and she squinted at Bashir. "If you say everything is all Palestine and I say everything is the whole land of Israel, I don't think we'll get anywhere," she said. "We share a common destiny here. I truly believe that we are so deeply and closely related—culturally, historically, religiously, psychologically. And it's so clear to me that you and your people are holding the key to our true freedom. And I think we could also say, Bashir, that we hold the key to your freedom. It's a deep interdependence. How can we free the heart, form our own healing? Is this possible?"

For Dalia, the solution lay in two states, side by side—much as they had existed prior to the Six-Day War in 1967. The difference would be that alongside Israel would rise a peaceful, independent

Palestinian state. The Palestinians would have their right of return, but it would be limited to only a part of old Palestine.

Bashir believed that the solution lay instead in 1948 and the long-held dream of a return to a single, secular, democratic state. He had always understood Dalia's gesture of sharing the house in al-Ramla, and making it into a kindergarten or Open House for the town's Arab children, as an acknowledgment of his right of return, and, by extension, of the rights of all Palestinian people to go back to their homeland.

Dalia, on the contrary, saw Open House as the result of one choice made by one individual. "It's not an overall solution and it's not a political statement," she would say. This was her personal decision, Dalia would make clear, and not one that should be required of other Israelis.

Bashir said that he wished there were more people like Dalia.

"We couldn't find two people who disagree more on how to visualize the viability of this land," Dalia said. "And yet we are so deeply connected. And what connects us? The same thing that separates us. This land."

Bashir took Dalia's hand. "I was afraid for you to come here," he said.

"I wanted to come," Dalia replied.

They stood and looked at each other, shaking hands and smiling.

"Expect me any day, Dalia," Bashir said. "I am forbidden to go to Jerusalem. But expect that one day, I will show up at your door."

Bashir released Dalia's hand, waved goodbye from the landing, and went back into his office. Dalia walked slowly down the single flight of stairs toward the street in Ramallah.

"Our enemy," she said softly, "is the only partner we have."

Chapter 23
THE LEMON TREE

In 1998, the fiftieth anniversary of the War of Independence and the Catastrophe, the lemon tree died. It had been bearing fewer lemons in recent years, and by the spring of 1998, just two shriveled, hard-shelled lemons lay on the ground, the only physical evidence that the tree had ever borne fruit.

"This is the nature of things; things just die on this planet," Dalia said at the time. "Trees die standing."

For a couple of years, the teachers of the Arab kindergarten at Open House would hang balloons and ribbons on the branches of the old lemon tree to help the children discern one color from another. The ribbons fluttered in the wind. Eventually a storm blew the tree down, leaving only a thick, gnarled stump.

Dalia hoped that one day Bashir and other Khairis could return to the house in Ramla to plant another lemon tree, as a sign of renewal.

On January 25, 2005, as a full moon rose over the coastal plain just east of the Mediterranean Sea, Dalia walked with a group of

Arab and Jewish teenagers to a corner of the garden at the house. In their hands was a lemon tree sapling. A cone of earth in the shape of a bucket clung to the sapling's roots. "It looked so fragile," Dalia said.

It was Tu B'shvat, the day Jewish sages call the holiday of the new year for trees. One of the Jewish teenagers had spontaneously suggested that this would be the perfect day to plant a new lemon tree.

"For years I was postponing this to wait for the Khairis," Dalia said. "And at that moment, the holiday of the trees, it felt so right, and yes, it's a new generation. And now the children will plant their tree in their house."

Dalia's hands, and the hands of the Arabs and of the Jews, lowered the sapling into a hole beside the old stump. They all went to the kitchen and brought a pail of water, and everyone gently tamped down the soil.

"I felt that the Khairis were not there, so there was something missing," Dalia recalled. "But that empty space was filled up with all these children. The trunk was there, very beautiful. Just by it, we planted a new sapling. I couldn't just let the past stay like that. Like a commemoration stone, the kind you put in a graveyard. The pain of our history.

"This dedication is without obliterating the memories. Something is growing out of the old history. Out of the pain, something new is growing.

"I wonder how they will take it," Dalia said of the Khairis. "It meant moving on. It meant it's the next generation now that's going to create a reality. That we are entrusting something in their hands. We are entrusting both the old and the new."

In the end, the decision of what to plant, and when, and where, was Dalia's. Bashir, when he heard about it by telephone, said he was pleased. Perhaps someday, he said, he would be back home in al-Ramla, and on that day, he would see the tree for himself.

AFTERWORD

At one o'clock on an April morning in 2011, a beam of light awakened Bashir Khairi in his Ramallah apartment. At first Bashir thought he was dreaming. Then he groggily concluded that the electricity was out and that his daughter, now twenty-five, was shining a flashlight into his bedroom. Suddenly wide awake, Bashir understood the source of the light. A contingent of Israeli special forces soldiers had raided the family home, breaching locked doors in the lobby and the upper floor where the family lived.

Bashir squinted into the light. One of the twenty black-masked soldiers was shining a high beam into his eyes in the bedroom, where moments before, Bashir had been sleeping beside his wife.

"You're Bashir," a commander barked. "We want you."

Bashir, sixty-nine years old, began to dress. His daughter was screaming, he recalled, so the soldiers taped her mouth shut. The commander ordered his men to seize the family's two computers, their mobile phones, and the memory chips on their cameras. The special forces spent two hours combing the apartment, yanking open drawers, cabinets, and closets. At 3:00 a.m. the soldiers took Bashir into the rainy night. Like the other times since he was first arrested forty-four years earlier, his family members didn't know where he was being taken or when they would see him again.

Bashir, handcuffed and blindfolded, rode with soldiers in the back of an army jeep. Their destination was an Israeli military base in the nearby settlement of Beit El, which had been established four decades earlier on lands confiscated from the Palestinian municipality of Al Bireh. Bashir's arrest was part of a broad sweep of suspected leaders and activists of the Popular Front for the Liberation of Palestine, which the Israeli intelligence agency, Shin Bet, suspected of plotting to kidnap Israeli soldiers and attack settlers. A few weeks earlier, an Israeli family in the West Bank settlement of Itamar had been brutally murdered, and the authorities had linked the crime to two PFLP members near the West Bank town of Nablus.

At the military base, intelligence officers brought Bashir into an interrogation room and handcuffed him to an armless metal chair bolted to the floor. One by one, he recalled later, five different officers questioned him.

"The order to arrest you has been signed by the chief of the Shin Bet," the agents told him. "Your activities jeopardize the security of Israel."

"I am a Palestinian who believes in the Palestinian cause," Bashir replied, repeating the words he had uttered over decades of interrogations. "And I despise the occupation. The crux of the Palestinian cause is the right of return. Otherwise there will be endless bloodshed."

For four days the questioning continued. Agents asked the same questions, and Bashir gave the same answers. After a while he told his questioner, "You're on the verge of making one of two decisions.

You'll either accuse me of a big crime, or you'll kill me. Concerning the first issue, I have nothing to confess. On the second question, I will make it easy for you. Life is like death for me. I don't care."

Presently a new Shin Bet agent, the deputy of the chief interrogator, came to take his turn. Bashir later recalled his name as Solli. He remembered a Solli from his family's past: a Jewish man who, in 1936, had helped his father design the house in al-Ramla. Perhaps this man from the Shin Bet was old Mr. Solli's grandson.

Agent Solli revealed that he and some of the other agents had read a book chronicling the story of Dalia and Bashir, and that they had been touched by the connection between two longtime enemies.

"He wanted to get to know me," Bashir remembered. "They were so happy and excited to meet the character in the book. They were really happy that I built a friendship with Dalia."

"Despite what you have said," said the agent, "we are still touched by the book."

"Unfortunately you don't understand the message of the book," Bashir said, still cuffed to the chair. Dalia had struggled to come to grips with the meaning of Palestinian dispossession, and had taken her own personal steps to help make amends. "Dalia was the only one in Israel who understood," Bashir insisted.

There was a pause. "I am aware of your history in Europe," Bashir said.

"So you recognize the Holocaust?" Solli asked.

"Yes. But," Bashir added, "you have gone from the victims to the victimizers."

After four days, mostly without sleep, and mostly cuffed to the chair, Bashir was allowed to go home. The Shin Bet did not charge him. When he returned, Bashir learned that each night since the soldiers took him, his daughter had awakened to her own screams.

"Chocolates?" Bashir's wife offers, extending a long box with different shapes in crinkled papers. She serves sweet Arabic tea from small etched glasses.

It is the summer of 2013. Bashir, in a blue button-down shirt and khakis, his left hand in his pocket, has been recounting the story of his latest arrest and interrogation, two years earlier. His hair has gone completely gray, matching his steel-framed glasses. His paunch is a bit larger.

Bashir and his visitor sit on a pair of sand-colored couches, in a pristine living room partially darkened by electronic blinds that block the late-afternoon sun. Bashir moved here, to an upscale Ramallah apartment building, a few years earlier. He chose an upper floor so that he could see Jerusalem, seven miles to the south. He is not allowed to visit, but he gazes at its spires every day.

In recent years, Bashir says, a stream of foreigners have come to see him, asking him how he is doing and whether he is still in touch with Dalia. "I haven't seen her in a long time," Bashir replies—not since 2005. They do talk occasionally, he says: *How are you? How is the family?* That sort of thing.

"But we haven't gone into things very deeply. It cooled off." Bashir pauses. "She was courageous at a time when the situation was difficult. But she retreated. I don't understand."

On an end table sits a model of the Al Aqsa mosque that, long ago, Bashir fashioned from two thousand pieces of silk and balsa wood while in prison in Jenin. He gestures toward the half-closed blinds, stands up, opens the door to the terrace, and walks outside. To the south stands Jerusalem, out of reach. Bashir looks toward it in silence.

A few days later, about ten miles southwest of Bashir's Ramallah apartment, Dalia sits on the second-floor terrace of an old Arab house, now converted to an upscale Israeli restaurant, in the formerly Palestinian village of Ein Karem, at the western edge of Jerusalem. Ein Karem is close to Dalia's West Jerusalem apartment, and she likes to come here from time to time, for its beauty and its history. Near sunset on a July evening, she looks west. The Judean Hills, as she calls them, soft and verdant, slope down toward a wide coastal plain, stretching to the Mediterranean. Partially hidden in their folds are a convent, and the gold domes of a Russian Orthodox church. Nearer, in the village itself, stands an old mosque, and a Catholic church at the place where Christians believe John the Baptist was born. The Virgin Mary is said to have visited here. Until July 1948, when Ein Karem was depopulated during the war, this was a Palestinian village, and its nearby fields were planted with olives, fruit trees, and vineyards. Now the village is home to Israeli artists and serves as a center for tourism. Three million people, including many Christian pilgrims, come to visit each year.

Dalia examines the menu: charred eggplant, beef carpaccio, duck risotto. She orders fish. The sound of an oud and rhythmic clapping drifts up to the terrace from the old mosque next door. A group of Palestinian travelers has just arrived at the mosque, and they are singing. They are mostly young observant Muslims, the men dressed in casual weekend Western clothes, the women in hijabs and abayas. Dalia looks up delightedly and joins the rhythmic clapping. "This is so wonderful," she says to her dinner companion. "Oh, yes, those are Muslims! I'm so happy! Why don't you go down there and ask them about why they're here?" The dinner companion comes back to report that most of them live in East Jerusalem in the Old City and that Ein Karem is one of many traditionally Palestinian places they have been visiting periodically. They met on Facebook and call themselves Qasdara, Arabic for "Walking." Every week, they go to the site of a different village that once stood in old Palestine. They want to try to reclaim, at least for moments, a sense of their broader homeland, and to show, in the words of their guide, that "what we can do is to be here. This land is not just belonging to Israelis."

"The serendipity is quite mind-blowing," Dalia says after learning of the group's mission. "I often ask myself questions about the memories of the places. For me it always has to do with the expansion of the heart. I find it a constant challenge to my own bias. For me it always confronts me with the story of the other."

For Dalia, confronting the story of the other began with Bashir. She asks about him, and within moments, she is in tears.

"He never answers my calls," Dalia cries. "I write him SMSs, I say happy holidays, he never replies. I wrote him a letter, he never answered. He doesn't even send me a card." Dalia dabs her eyes with a napkin. "I know intuitively that he thinks that I've changed over the last years, of course we all change all the time." Some of Bashir's bad feelings may be built on a misunderstanding. Bashir believes Dalia violated their agreement to keep the kindergarten in Ramle exclusively for Arab children, but Dalia says this is wrong. "If something is being projected on me which is not true that's not fair," she laments, crying again. Yet this alone, Dalia believes, does not explain Bashir's distance. She wonders aloud if Raphael's service in the Israel

Defense Forces upset Bashir but stresses that "we made sure he would be non-combat. He was a teacher in the army." Or perhaps, she says, Bashir's silence has to do with an Israeli friend of Bashir's, who came to Dalia a few years earlier, asking her to petition the city of Ramla to return the old Arab houses to their original Palestinian owners. "We cannot do this," she told the man. "We're trying to draw the Jewish people in! You want to threaten their houses? Half the city is sitting in Arab houses."

Dalia understood that Bashir was sending a personal appeal to her, through a messenger, to endorse the Palestinian right of return and to help Bashir "unite his hand to the land." Yet for Dalia, that would mean "that now I will go around Israel and ask people to leave their homes and return it to the Palestinians. No, I'm not going to do that, that's not my purpose." Whether or not the man was delivering a hidden message from Bashir, the proposal went far beyond the personal decision that Dalia had made decades earlier to share the Ramla home, as best she could, with the Khairi family. Bashir's friend was proposing an "unthinkable" step, Dalia said, one she felt it was impossible to take.

In some ways, the specifics of Bashir's decision to maintain silence with Dalia do not matter. They are symptomatic of a steady deterioration of relations between Israelis and Palestinians, as Israel claims ever more West Bank land, the settler population surpasses 800,000, and seventeen Israeli settlements encircle East Jerusalem, long the place Palestinians fought for as the capital of their new nation of Palestine. Now, special roads just for settlers and "VIPs" criss-cross the West Bank. Palestinians are not allowed on these roads—even though they, too, were built on lands supposedly set aside for a future Palestine. The vast majority of these radical changes to the landscape occurred despite the "peace process" that began in 1993. Hundreds of checkpoints and other barriers continue to dot occupied Palestinian land, and Israeli military forces retain control of 60 percent of the West Bank and of Gaza by air and sea. Many Palestinians are cut off from their families, their freedom of movement severely curtailed. Palestinians spend hours waiting at military checkpoints to get to work or to visit family and friends. They are unable to travel to Jerusalem to pray at ancient holy sites, since it is now part of a "unified" Israeli capital and off limits to most Palestinians.

Since Dalia and Bashir last saw each other, in 2005, multiple wars have devastated Gaza, killing more than 3,200 Palestinian civilians, including more than one thousand children, mostly killed by Israeli air strikes. During that same time, twenty-nine Israeli civilians died from Hamas rocket attacks launched from Gaza. None of those were children. Yet, despite the dramatic disparity in casualties, throughout Israel, and in the media, Palestinians are often portrayed as the aggressors, and Israelis, the victims. And so, as Israelis become more fearful, and their leaders seize ever more land to expand settlements, the prospects of a just peace agreement grow smaller and smaller.

As Palestinians watched their land base shrink, teams of Israeli and American peace negotiators demanded that they accept the "solution" of a shrunken, fragmented homeland, broken into smaller pieces by Israeli settlements and surrounded by military forces. Palestinians are told they must give up their dream of a national capital in East Jerusalem and accept that Gaza will be permanently severed from the West Bank, isolating the two populations from each other and from East Jerusalem. Under these proposals, Israel would retain military control around Palestinian borders and even control the precious underground water lying beneath Palestinian cities and towns. Despite internal divisions among Palestinians, they united in rejecting these proposals, considering them no less than surrender. From a younger generation, new ideas emerged, highlighting non-violent means for Palestinians to change the reality in their homeland.

Dalia tried to stay hopeful, and to act accordingly, especially through Open House. She pressed forward: with the kindergarten for Arab children in Ramla, and with Arab-Jewish dialogue through encounter groups and a summer camp, including an especially emotional camp session of Arab and Jewish children during the Gaza war in the summer of 2014. Despite these efforts, Bashir, like many Palestinians, has come to believe the "peace process," with its characteristic dialogue groups, has only led to greater Palestinian confinement. Increasingly, the struggle for Palestinian freedom has led to direct nonviolent resistance, including a growing "BDS" movement, for Boycott, Divestment, and Sanctions, to apply international pressure on Israel to end the occupation and recognize Palestinian rights. The time for dialogue and encounter groups, many Palestinians believe, has long since passed.

Yet Dalia, on the terrace of the former Arab house, next to the old mosque in Ein Karem, cannot accept Bashir's silence. "He was born from the same home that I was born from, we emanate from the same place," she says, her hands clasped together, pressing up against her chin. "If people like me and Bashir who sustained against all odds a friendship . . ." She pauses. "It's deeper than friendship."

Dalia looks west, above the darkening hills, at Venus hanging in the evening sky. She weeps softly.

"It has something to do with family," she says.

ABOUT THE RESEARCH
FOR THIS BOOK

This book is an adaptation for young readers of an adult book that first published in 2006. The adaptation was completed with the help of authors Rich Wallace and Sandra Neil Wallace. Many thanks for their excellent work. The seed for the original book was a forty-three-minute radio documentary I produced for National Public Radio's *Fresh Air* in 1998 on the fiftieth anniversary of the 1948 Arab-Israeli war. All else flowed from there.

This book is entirely a work of nonfiction. While many of the events described happened decades ago, their retelling is based on interviews, archival documents, published and unpublished memoirs, newspaper clippings, and primary and secondary historical accounts.

In rare cases, I have described an event based on multiple interviews with family members who are recounting family oral history or who describe the customs of the family that would have led to the events described. In those cases, I have indicated so in the text. Crucial and more controversial moments in each family's history rely strictly on the aforementioned documents and eyewitness accounts.

In some cases old memories clash: Nuha Khairi, for example,

specifically recalls Dalia being at the house in al-Ramla on the day her father, Ahmad, came to the door in 1969; Dalia is certain she was not there that day. In such cases I describe both the conflict in memory and the common ground of agreement. Dalia and Bashir also differ, and agree, on places and times each was present: where there is difference in memory or argument, I either eliminated the portions that didn't match or noted them.

Dalia and Bashir reviewed the original adult book for accuracy, as have numerous scholars and experts, both Israeli and Palestinian. In addition, that manuscript underwent a rigorous, monthslong fact-checking process, in which thousands of facts were checked against interview transcripts, historical texts, memoirs, archival documents, and other material. This edition was entirely adapted from that work. Any mistakes that may remain are, of course, my responsibility.

TO LEARN MORE

Since *The Lemon Tree* was first published in 2006, I've had the good fortune to travel widely to discuss its message and to document the distressing changes in the Holy Land and the difficulties of staying hopeful as a just peace becomes more and more elusive. Yet, in my appearances in churches, mosques, synagogues, universities, and bookstores, in my talks from Ramallah and Jerusalem to Paris, New York, Los Angeles, Seattle, Milwaukee, St. Louis, villages and towns all across America, and even book clubs in Egypt and Saudi Arabia, via Skype, one thing remains clear: the story of this profound and difficult friendship between Dalia and Bashir continues to resonate. Through their connection, politicians, diplomats, scholars, military leaders, and most of all, ordinary people, see in these two old friends the power of hope for a better day.

Over the years, many people have approached me with suggestions for additional reading or to recommend a film or series of newspaper articles. There's a big bibliography, starting on page 173, but here I'm providing suggestions for additional books, articles, and films you might enjoy. This is a random list of some of my personal favorites.

Most of these have come out since the original *Lemon Tree* was published. The films are mostly available on YouTube, Amazon, or Netflix.

BOOKS AND ARTICLES

Mourid Barghouti, *I Saw Ramallah*. A Palestinian poet returns home after the 1993 peace accords.

Ibrahim Fawal, *On the Hills of God*, a little-known but captivating novel of the Palestinian "Nakba," following three young friends.

David Grossman, *To the End of the Land*, a novel about a mother and her son, an Israeli soldier, by the bestselling Israeli novelist.

Yoram Kaniuk, *1948: A Novel* (translated by Anthony Berris), by the Israeli writer and veteran of the 1948 war.

Mark LeVine and Mathias Mossberg, eds., *One Land, Two States*, about "parallel states," an unconventional solution to the long tragedy of Israel and Palestine.

Edward W. Said, *The End of the Peace Process: Oslo and After,* and *Reflections on Exile and Other Essays*, by the late Palestinian writer and intellectual and professor at Columbia.

Raja Shehadeh, *Palestinian Walks: Forays into a Vanishing Landscape*, a beautiful account of one man's quest to continue his tradition of long walks in his homeland, despite the occupation.

Avi Shlaim, *Israel and Palestine: Reappraisals, Revisions, Refutations*, by the Israeli-born professor of history at Oxford. His book *The Iron Wall: Israel and the Arab World* is an excellent historical account of political divisions within Israel.

Sandy Tolan, *Children of the Stone: The Power of Music in a Hard Land*, my book about a Palestinian musician and his dream to build a music school in occupied Palestine.

You can also find my recent writings at sandytolan.com. For specific ideas on resolutions beyond the fading "two-state solution," search for "What Comes Next? A Forum on the End of the Two-State Paradigm" (*Mondoweiss*), Ian Lustick's "Two-State Illusion" (*New York Times*), "There Will Be a One-State Solution" by Yousef Munayyer (*Foreign Affairs*), my commentary, "For Arab and Jew, a New Beginning" (*Christian Science Monitor*), and the groundbreaking work by Peter Beinart, "I No Longer Believe in a Jewish State" (*New York Times*). Nathan Thrall's excellent work in the *New York Times* and *New York Review of Books* helps explain the current situation. For an American Jewish, mostly pro-Israel perspective, try *The Forward*. For pro-Palestinian views, try *Mondoweiss* or *The Electronic Intifada*. It's also helpful to read work from outside the U.S. This includes the Israeli newspaper *Ha'aretz*, including the columns of Gideon Levy, Bradley Burston, Amira Hass, and Diana Buttu, whose work is widely published and searchable. Though based in Washington, *Al-Monitor* provides news and analysis from across the Middle East. *Al Jazeera* is another good source for perspectives outside the U.S., as is *The Guardian*, from London.

FILM AND TELEVISION

5 Broken Cameras, a 2011 film by Emad Burnat and Guy Davidi, about a Palestinian village's resistance to Israeli occupation. Nominated for an Academy Award for best documentary.

Amreeka, a 2009 film by Cherien Dabis, about a Palestinian woman who emigrates to the U.S. with her teenage son.

Budrus, a 2009 film by Julia Bacha about the nonviolent resistance of one Palestinian village.

Foxtrot, a 2017 film by Samuel Maoz about a mother and father's loss of their son, a soldier in the Israeli army.

The Gatekeepers, a 2012 film by Dror Moreh about Israel's occupation of Palestinian lands, told through the perspective of former Israeli intelligence officials.

The Promise, a 2011 series from the BBC, about a young woman who travels to Israel/Palestine, retracing the steps of her grandfather, a British soldier in the Holy Land in the days just before Israel was born.

Promises, a 2001 documentary by B.Z. Goldberg, which examines the conflict through the perspective of seven Israeli and Palestinian children.

Speed Sisters, a 2015 documentary by Amber Fares about Palestinian women race car drivers.

Waltz with Bashir, a 2008 animated documentary by Ari Folman about Israel's war in Lebanon.

SOURCES

ARCHIVES

American Jewish Joint Distribution Committee Archives. Queens, New York, and Jerusalem, Israel.

Broadcast Archives of the British Broadcasting Corporation. London.

The Central Zionist Archives. Jerusalem, Israel.

Institute for Palestinian Studies Archives. Beirut, Lebanon.

Israel State Archives. Jerusalem, Israel.

Kibbutz Na'an Archives. Kibbutz Na'an, Israel.

Lyndon Baines Johnson Library Archives. Austin, Texas.

National Archives of Bulgaria. Sofia, Bulgaria.

National Archives of the United States. Washington, D.C.

National Library of Bulgaria. Sofia, Bulgaria.

Palestinian Association for Cultural Exchange. Ramallah, West Bank.

ELECTRONIC SOURCES (INCLUDING ONLINE MEDIA)

"A Small Revolution in Ramle." *Ha'aretz.* http://www.haaretzdaily.com/hasen/pages/ShArt.jhtml?itemNo=337040&contrassID = 2&subContrassID = 5&sbSubContrassID=0&listSrc=Y.

"Background of the Repatriation and Land Exportation Schemes and the Laws Purporting to Justify Israel's Actions." http://www.badil.org/Publications/Legal_Papers/cescr-2003-A1.pdf.

Bard, Dr. Mitchell. "Myth and Fact: The Creation of Hamas." *United Jewish Communities: The Federations of North America.* http://www.ujc.org /content_display.html?ArticleID=114644.

Bodendorfer, Gerhard. "Jewish Voices About Jesus." *Jewish-Christian Relations.* http://www.jcrelations.net/en/?id=738.

"Count Folke Bernadotte." Jewish Virtual Library. http://www .jewishvirtuallibrary.org/jsource/biography/Bernadotte.html.

"Giuliani: 'Thank God That George Bush Is Our President.'" CNN. http://www .cnn.com/2004/ALLPOLITICS/08/30/giuliani.transcript/index.html.

"Gregorian-Hijri Dates Converter." June 7, 2005. http://www.rabiah.com /convert/convert.php3.

"Hezbollah Fires Rockets into Northern Israel." CNN. http://www.cnn.com /WORLD/9603/israel_lebanon/30/.

"Interview with Defense Minister Arens on Israel Television—8 May 1983." Israel Ministry of Foreign Affairs. http://www.mfa.gov.il/MFA /Foreign+Relations/Israels+Foreign+Relations+since+1947/1982– 1984/111+Interview+with+Defense+Minister+Arens+on+Israe.htm.

"Israel 1948–1967: Why Was King Abdullah of Jordan Assassinated in 1951?" Palestine Facts. http://www.palestinefacts.org/pf_1948to1967_abdulla.php.

"Israel Sends Letter to UN Protesting Hezbollah Attack." *Ha'aretz.* http://www .haaretz.com/hasen/pages/ShArt.jhtml?itemNo=436197&contrassID=13.

"Israeli Army Blows Up Palestinian Broadcasting Center." CNN. http://archives .cnn.com/2002/WORLD/meast/01/18/mideast.violence.

"Israeli West Bank Barrier." Wikipedia. http://en.wikipedia.org/wiki /Israeli_West_Bank_barrier.

"John Kerry: Strengthening Israel's Security." Jewish Virtual Library. http:// www.jewishvirtuallibrary.org/jsource/US-Israel/kerryisrael.html.

"Knowledge Bank: Profiles—Gamel Abdel Nasser." CNN. http://www.cnn.com /SPECIALS/cold.war/kbank/profiles/nasser.

"Lebanese Mortar Lands in Northern Israel." http://archives.tcm.ie /breakingnews/2005/08/25/story217788.asp.

Meron, Ya'akov. "Why Jews Fled the Arab Countries." http://www.freerepublic .com/focus/f-news/956344/posts.

"Moroccan Jewish Immigration to Israel." http://rickgold.home.mindspring .com/Emigration/emigration%20statistics.htm.

"Moroccan Jews." http://www.usa-morocco.org/moroccan-jews.htm.

Pappe, Ilan. "Were They Expelled?—The History, Historiography and Relevance of the Palestinian Refugee Problem." http://www.nakbainhebrew.org /library/were_they_expelled.rtf

"PLO Founder Killed by Israeli Missile Attack." News.telegraph. http://www .telegraph.co.uk/news/main.jhtml?xml=/news/2001/08/28/wmid28.xml.

"Progress Report of the United Nations Mediator on Palestine." UNISPAL. http://domino.un.org / UNISPAL.NSF /0 /cc33602f61b0935c80256 48800368307? Open Document.

"Progress Report of the United Nations Mediator on Palestine Submitted to the Secretary-General for Transmission to the Members of the United Nations." UNISPAL. http://domino.un.org/UNISPAL.NSF/0/ab14d4aafc4e1bb9852562 04004f55fa?OpenDocument.

Remnick, David. "Profiles: The Spirit Level: Amos Oz Writes the Story of Israel." *The New Yorker*. http://www.newyorker.com/fact/content/?041108fa _fact.

Shlaim, Avi. "Israel and the Arab Coalition in 1948." Cambridge University Press. http://www.fathom.com/course/72810001.

"The Law of Return 5710 (1950)." Knesset. http://www.knesset.gov.il/laws /special/eng/return.htm.

"The Making of Transjordan." Hashemite Kingdom of Jordan. http://www .kinghussein.gov.jo/his_transjordan.html.

"The Separation Barrier in the West Bank." B'tselem. September 2005. http:// www.btselem.org/Download/Separation_Barrier_Map_Eng.pdf.

"Water and the Arab-Israeli Conflict." http://www.d-n-i.net/al_aqsa_intifada /collins_water.htm.

"Why Did Arabs Reject the Proposed UN GA Partition Plan Which Split Palestine into Jewish and Arab States?" Palestine Remembered. http:// www.palestineremembered.com/Acre/Palestine-Remembered/Story448 .html.

Yacobi, Haim. "From Urban Panopticism to Spatial Protests: Housing Policy, Segregation, and Social Exclusion of the Palestinian Community in the City of Lydda-Lod." 2001. http://www.lincolninst.edu/pubs/dl/622_yacobi.pdf.

Zureik, Elia. "Palestinian Refugees and the Peace Process." http://www.arts .mcgill.ca/MEPP/PrrN/papers/Zureik2.html

NEWSPAPER AND MAGAZINE ARTICLES IN PRINT

"2 Die, 8 Wounded in J'lem Terror Outrage at Supersol." *Jerusalem Post*, February 23, 1969.

Amos, Elon. "War Without End." *New York Review*, July 15, 2004.

"Anglican Clergyman, Surgeon, Among Those Held in Terrorist Round-Up." *Jerusalem Post*, March 4, 1969.

Bellos, Susan. "Supersol Victims Buried; Allon Promises Vengeance." *Jerusalem Post*, February 24, 1969.

Bilby, Kenneth. "Israeli Tanks Take Arab Air Base at Lydda." *New York Herald Tribune*, July 11, 1948.

——. "Israeli Units Cut Way into Ramle, Lydda Surrender of Both Reported in Cairo." *New York Herald Tribune*, July 12, 1948.

Currivan, Gene. "Arabs Encircled at Vital Highway, Surrender Lydda." *The New York Times*, July 12, 1948.

——. "Curb Arabs, Count Bids UN; Israeli Force Wins Ramleh." *The New York Times*, July 13, 1948.

Feron, James. "Bomb Explosion in Jerusalem's Largest Supermarket Kills 2, Injures 9." *The New York Times*, February 22, 1969.

——. "Israel and Arabs: Tensions in the Occupied Territories." *The New York Times*, April 28, 1968.

"First Sabotage Attempt on Supersol Failed." *Jerusalem Post*, May 14, 1969.

" 'Front' Chief Says Terrorism Against Israel to Continue." *Jerusalem Post*, March 5, 1969.

"Houses of 9 West Bank Terrorists Demolished." *Jerusalem Post*, March 11, 1969.

Safadi, Anan, and Malka Rabinowitz. "Major Terror Gang Seized." *Jerusalem Post*, March 6, 1969.

"Supersol." *Jerusalem Post*, February 23, 1969.

"Supersol Blast Suspects Held in Round-up of 40." *Jerusalem Post*, March 2, 1969.

"Supersol Crime Reconstructed." *Jerusalem Post*, March 3, 1969.

"Supersol Reopens; Business as Usual." *Jerusalem Post*, February 24, 1969.

JOURNALS AND JOURNAL ARTICLES

Abu Hadba, Abdul Aziz, ed. *Society and Heritage* 32 (1998).

Abukhalil, As'ad. "George Habash and the Movement of Arab Nationalists: Neither Unity Nor Liberation." *Journal of Palestine Studies* (1999).

Abu Sitta, Salman. "Special Report of Badil: Quantification of Land Confiscated inside the Green Line." *Annex to Follow-Up Information Submitted to the Committee for Economic, Social and Cultural Rights* (2000).

Alpher, Joseph, and Khalil Shikaki. "Concept Paper: The Palestinian Refugee Problem and the Right of Return." *Middle East Policy* 6 (1999): 167–189.

Bruhns, Fred C. "A Study of Arab Refugee Attitudes." *Middle East Journal* 9 (1955): 130–38.

Busailah, Reja-E. "The Fall of Lydda, 1948: Impressions and Reminiscences." *Arab Studies Quarterly* 3 (1981): 123–51.

Christison, Kathleen. "Bound by a Frame of Reference, Part II: U.S. Policy and the Palestinians, 1948–1988." *Journal of Palestine Studies* (1998).

Friedman, Adina. "Unraveling the Right of Return." *Refugee* 21 (2003).

Gilmour, David. "The 1948 Arab Exodus." *Middle East International* 286 (1986): 13–14.

Hanafi, Sari. "Opening the Debate on the Right of Return." *Middle East Report: War Without Borders* 2–7.

Hanieh, Akram. "The Camp David Papers." *Journal of Palestine Studies* 2 (2001): 75–97.

Khader, Hassan. "Confessions of a Palestinian Returnee." *Journal of Palestine Studies* 27 (1997).

Khalidi, Walid. "Selected Documents on the 1948 Palestine War." *Journal of Palestine Studies* 27 (1998): 60–105.

Lebanese Center for Documentation and Research, ed. "Political Violence in the World: 1967–1987." *Chronology Bibliography Documents*, Vol. 1. Beirut: 1988.

Lesch, Ann M. "Israeli Deportation of Palestinians from the West Bank and the Gaza Strip, 1967–1978." *Journal of Palestine Studies* 8 (1979): 101–31.

Macpherson, Rev. James Rose, trans. *Palestine Pilgrims Text Society* 3 (1895).

———. *Palestine Pilgrims Text Society* 5 (1895).

———. *Palestine Pilgrims Text Society* 6 (1895).

———. *Palestine Pilgrims Text Society* 8 (1895).

Middle East International (various biweekly issues, 2003–2005).

Morris, Benny. "Operation Dani and the Palestinian Exodus from Lydda and Ramle in 1948." *Middle East Journal* 40 (1986): 82–109.

———. "The Causes and Character of the Arab Exodus from Palestine: The Israel Defense Forces Intelligence Branch Analysis of June 1948." *Middle Eastern Studies* 22 (1986): 5–19.

Munayyer, Spiro, and Walid Khalidi. "Special Document: The Fall of Lydda." *Journal of Palestine Studies* 27 (1998): 80–98.

Palestine-Israel Journal of Politics Economics and Culture 9, no. 4 (2002). *Narratives of 1948*. East Jerusalem: Middle East Publications, 2002.

"Palestinian Refugees of Lebanon Speak." *Journal of Palestine Studies* 26 (1995): 54–60.

Said, Edward W. "A Changing World Order." *Arab Studies Quarterly* 3 (1981).

Social, Cultural, and Educational Association of the Jews in the People's Republic of Bulgaria 14 (1983).

"Special Document: Israel and Torture." *Journal of Palestine Studies* 9 (1977): 191–219.

Tamari, Salim, ed. *Jerusalem Quarterly File* (2003).

Yost, Charles. "The Arab-Israeli War: How It Began." *Foreign Affairs* (January 1968). Vol. 46, no. 2.

PUBLISHED ARTICLES AND PAMPHLETS

"Aufruf/Ma'amar: Article." Hulda Takam Archive, 1947 or 1948.

"Deportation of Palestinians from the Occupied Territories and the Mass Deportation of December 1992." Jerusalem: Israeli Information Center for Human Rights in the Occupied Territories (B'Tselem), 1993.

Masalha, Nur. "The 1967 Palestinian Exodus." *The Palestinian Exodus* 1948–1998. Ghada Karmi and Eugene Cotran, eds. London: Ithaca Press, 1999.

Mossek, Moshe. "The Struggle for the Leadership Among the Jews of Bulgaria Following Liberation." *Eastern European Jewry—From Holocaust to Redemption*, 1944–1948. Benjamin Pinkus, ed. Sede Boqer, Israel: Ben-Gurion University Press, 1987.

Paounovski, Vladimir. "The Anti-Jewish Legislation in Bulgaria During the Second World War." From *The Jews in Bulgaria between the Holocaust and the Rescue*. Sofia: Adasa-Pres, 2000.

Pappe, Ilan. "Were They Expelled?: The History, Historiography and Relevance of the Palestinian Refugee Problem." *The Palestinian Exodus* 1948–1998. Ghada Karmi and Eugene Cotran, eds. London: Ithaca Press, 1999.

GOVERNMENT PUBLICATIONS

A Survey of Palestine: Prepared in December 1945 and January 1946 for the Information of the Anglo-American Committee of Inquiry. Jerusalem: The Government Printer, 1946.

Great Britain. Labour Middle East Council, Conservative Middle East Council, Liberal Democratic Middle East Council. Joint Parliamentary Middle East Councils Commission of Enquiry—Palestinian Refugees, Right of Return. London, 2001.

Israel. State of Israel. Government Year Book 5714 (1953–1954). Government Printer.

Palestine and Transjordan Administration Reports 1918–1948 (vols. 5, 6, 10, and 16), archive editions, 1995.

Ramla City Council Minutes. Ramla, Israel, 1949.

United Nations. United Nations Relief and Works Agency (UNRWA). *UNRWA: The Long Journey* 45 (1993).

United Nations. United Nations Special Committee on Palestine. *Report on Palestine: Report to the General Assembly by the United Nations Special Committee on Palestine.* New York: Somerset Books, 1947.

MEDIA

Journey to Jerusalem. Ivan Nichev, director. Videocassette. Bulgarian National Television, 2003.

The Lemon Tree. Sandy Tolan, producer. NPR's Fresh Air, 1998.

The Optimists: The Story of the Rescue of the Bulgarian Jews from the Holocaust. Jacky Comforty, director. Videocassette. New Day Films, 2001.

Troubled Waters. Sandy Tolan, producer. A five-part series for NPR's Living on Earth. Portions aired on NPR's Weekend Edition, 1997.

UNPUBLISHED WORKS

Alkalay, Iris. "My Father's Three Bulgarias."

Chapple, John. "Jewish Land Settlement in Palestine" (unpublished paper), 1964.

Krispin, Alfred. "The Rescue of the Jews in Bulgaria: A Closely Kept Secret. Recollections of a Bulgarian Jew."

"The Jewish Community in Plovdiv: History, Style of Living, Culture, Traditions, Place in the Life of the Town."

BOOKS

Abdul Hadi, Mahdi F. *Palestine Documents Volume II: From the Negotiations in Madrid to the Post–Hebron Agreement Period.* Jerusalem: PASSIA, 1997.

Abdulhadi, Faiha, ed. and compiler. *Bibliography of Palestinian Oral History (with a Special Focus on Palestinian Women).* Al-Bireh, West Bank: Palestinian National Authority Ministry of Planning and International Cooperation, 1999.

Abu Hussein, Hussein, and Fiona McKay. *Access Denied: Palestinian Land Rights in Israel.* London: Zed Books, 2003.

Abu Nowar, Maan. *The Jordanian-Israeli War: 1948–1951: A History of the Hashemite Kingdom of Jordan.* Reading, U.K.: Ithaca Press, 2002.

Aburish, Said K. *Arafat: From Defender to Dictator.* London: Bloomsbury, 1998.

Abu-Sharif, Bassam, and Uzi Mahnaimi. *Best of Enemies.* Boston: Little, Brown & Co., 1995.

Ajami, Fouad. *The Arab Predicament: Arab Political Thought and Practice Since 1967.* Cambridge: Cambridge University Press, 1992.

———. *The Dream Palace of the Arabs: A Generation's Odyssey.* New York: Vintage Books, 1998.

Almog, Oz. *The Sabra: The Creation of the New Jew.* Translated by Haim Watzman. Berkeley, Calif: University of California Press, 2000.

Amad, Adnan, ed. *Israeli League for Human and Civil Rights.* Beirut: Neebii.

Anidjar, Gil. *The Jew, the Arab: A History of the Enemy.* Stanford, Calif.: Stanford University Press, 2003.

Armstrong, Karen. *Jerusalem: One City, Three Faiths.* New York: Ballantine Books, 1996.

Aruri, Naseer. *Dishonest Broker: The Role of the United States in Palestine and Israel.* Cambridge, Mass.: South End Press, 2003.

———. *Palestinian Refugees: The Right of Return.* London: Pluto Press, 2001.

Avineri, Shlomo. *The Making of Modern Zionism: The Intellectual Origins of the Jewish State.* New York: Basic Books, 1981.

Avishai, Bernard. *Tragedy of Zionism: How Its Revolutionary Past Haunts Israeli Democracy.* New York: Helios Press, 2002.

Bahour, Sam, and Alice Lynd, eds. *Homeland: Oral Histories of Palestine and Palestinians.* New York: Olive Branch Press, 1994.

Bar-Gal, Yoram. *Propaganda and Zionist Education: The Jewish National Fund 1924–1947.* Rochester, N.Y.: University of Rochester Press, 2003.

Bar-Joseph, Uri. *The Best of Enemies: Israel and Transjordan in the War of 1948.* London: Frank Cass, 1987.

Bar-Zohar, Michael. *Beyond Hitler's Grasp: The Heroic Rescue of Bulgaria's Jews.* Holbrook, Mass.: Adams Media Corporation, 1998.

Barouh, Emmy. *Jews in the Bulgarian Lands: Ancestral Memory and Historical Destiny.* Sofia: Inernational Center for Minority Studies and Intercultural Relations, 2001.

Bauer, Yehuda. *Out of the Ashes.* Oxford: Pergamon Press, 1989.

Begley, Louis. *Wartime Lies.* New York: Ballantine Books, 1991.

Bennis, Phyllis. *Understanding the Palestinian-Israeli Conflict.* Orlando, Fla.: TARI, 2002.

Ben-Sasson, H. H., ed. *A History of the Jewish People.* Cambridge, Mass.: Harvard University Press, 1976.

Bentwich, Norman. *Israel: Two Faithful Years, 1967–1969.* London: Elek Books Ltd., 1970.

Benvenisti, Meron. *Intimate Enemies: Jews and Arabs in a Shared Land.* Berkeley, Calif: University of California Press, 1995.

———. *Sacred Landscapes: The Buried History of the Holy Land Since 1948.* Berkeley, Calif.: University of California Press, 2000.

Bishara, Marwan. *Palestine/Israel: Peace or Apartheid—Prospects for Resolving the Conflict.* New York: Zed Books, 2001.

Bisharat, George Emile. *Palestinian Lawyers and Israeli Rule: Law and Disorder in the West Bank.* Austin: University of Texas Press, 1989.

Braizat, Musa S. *The Jordanian-Palestinian Relationship: The Bankruptcy of the Confederal Idea.* London: British Academic Press, 1998.

Brenner, Lenni. *The Iron Wall: Zionist Revisionism from Jabotinsky to Shamir.* London: Zed Books, 1984.

————. *Zionism in the Age of Dictators*. London: Croom Helm, 1983.

Bucaille, Laetitia. *Growing Up Palestinian: Israeli Occupation and the Intifada Generation*. Princeton, N.J.: Princeton University Press, 2004.

Carey, Roane, and Jonathan Shainin, eds. *The Other Israel: Voices of Refusal and Dissent*. New York: The New Press, 2002.

Chary, Frederick B. *The Bulgarian Jews and the Final Solution, 1940–1944*. Pittsburgh: University of Pittsburgh Press, 1972.

Childers, Erskine B. *The Road to Suez: A Study of Western-Arab Relations*. London: Macgibbon & Kee, 1962.

Cleveland, William. *History of the Modern Middle East*. Boulder, Colo.: Westview Press, 1994.

Cohen, Aharon. *Israel and the Arab World*. Boston: Beacon Press, 1976.

Cohen, David, compiler. *The Survival: A Compilation of Documents 1940–1944*. Sofia: "Shalom" Publishing Centre, 1944.

Cohen, H. J. *The Jews of the Middle East, 1860–1972*. Jerusalem: Israel Universities Press, 1973.

Cohen, Michael J. *Palestine and the Great Powers: 1945–1948*. Princeton, N.J.: Princeton University Press, 1982.

————. "The Anglo-American Committee on Palestine, 1945–1946." *The Rise of Israel*, vol. 35. New York: Garland Publishing, Inc., 1987.

————. "United Nations Discussions on Palestine, 1947." *The Rise of Israel*, vol. 37. New York: Garland Publishing, Inc., 1987.

————. "The Recognition of Israel, 1948." *The Rise of Israel*, vol. 39. New York: Garland Publishing, Inc., 1987.

Connell, Dan. *Rethinking Revolution: New Strategies for Democracy and Social Justice: The Experience of Eritrea, South Africa, Palestine, and Nicaragua*. Lawrenceville, N.J.: Red Sea Press, 2001.

Constant, Stephan. *Foxy Ferdinand: 1861–1948, Tsar of Bulgaria*. London: Sidgwick & Jackson, 1979.

Crampton, R. J. *A Short History of Modern Bulgaria*. Cambridge: Cambridge University Press, 1987.

Darwish, Mahmoud. *Memory for Forgetfulness: August, Beirut, 1982*. Translated from the Arabic by Ibrahim Muhawi. Berkeley, Calif.: University of California Press, 1995.

Dayan, Yael. *Israel Journal: June 1967.* New York: McGraw-Hill, 1967.

El-Asmar, Fouzi. *Through the Hebrew Looking-Glass: Arab Stereotypes in Children's Literature.* Vermont: Amana Books, 1986.

———. *To Be an Arab in Israel.* London: Frances Pinter Ltd., 1975.

Einstein, Albert. *About Zionism: Speeches and Letters.* Translated and edited with an introduction by Leon Simon. New York: Macmillan, 1931.

Elon, Amos. *A Blood-Dimmed Tide: Dispatches from the Middle East.* New York: Columbia University Press, 1997.

———. *The Israelis: Founders and Sons.* Tel Aviv: Adam Publishers, 1981.

———. *Jerusalem: City of Mirrors.* Boston: Little, Brown & Co., 1989.

Enderlin, Charles. *Shattered Dreams: The Failure of the Peace Process in the Middle East, 1995–2002.* Translated from the French by Susan Fairfield. New York: Other Press, 2003.

Eshkenazi, Jacques, and Alfred Krispin. *Jews in Bulgarian Hinterland: An Annotated Bibliography.* Translated from the Bulgarian by Alfred Krispin. Sofia: International Center for Minority Studies and Intercultural Relations, 2002.

Eveland, Wilbur Crane. *Ropes of Sand: America's Failure in the Middle East.* London: W. W. Norton & Co., 1980.

Farsoun, Samih K. *Palestine and the Palestinians.* Boulder, Colo.: Westview Press, 1997.

Feiler, Bruce. *Abraham: A Journey to the Heart of Three Faiths.* New York: William Morrow, 2002.

———. *Walking the Bible: A Journey by Land Through the Five Books of Moses.* New York: William Morrow, 2001.

Finkelstein, Israel, and Neil Asher Silberman. *The Bible Unearthed: Archaeology's New Vision of Ancient Israel and the Origin of Its Sacred Texts.* New York: Simon & Schuster, 2001.

Flapan, Simha. *The Birth of Israel: Myths and Realities.* New York: Pantheon Books, 1987.

Frances, Samuel. *Recuerdos Alegres, Recuerdos Tristes.* Sofia: Shalom, 2000.

Friedman, Thomas L. *From Beirut to Jerusalem.* New York: Anchor Books, 1995.

Gaff, Angela. *An Illusion of Legality: A Legal Analysis of Israel's Mass Deportation of Palestinians on 17 December 1992*. Ramallah: Al-Haq, 1993.

Gefen, Israel. *An Israeli in Lebanon*. London: Pickwick Books, 1986.

———. *Years of Fire*. London: Ferrington, 1995.

Gelber, Yoav. *Palestine 1948: War, Escape and Emergence of the Palestinian Refugee Problem*. Brighton: Sussex Academic Press, 2001.

Gerner, Deborah. *One Land, Two Peoples: The Conflict over Palestine*. Boulder, Colo.: Westview Press, 1994.

Gharaibeh, Fawzi A. *The Economies of the West Bank and Gaza Strip*. Boulder, Colo.: Westview Press, 1985.

Glubb, Sir John Bagot. *A Soldier with the Arabs*. London: Hodder & Stoughton, 1957.

Green, Stephen. *Taking Sides: America's Secret Relations with a Militant Israel, 1948–1967*. London: Faber & Faber, 1984.

Gresh, Alain. *The PLO, the Struggle Within: Towards an Independent Palestinian State*. Translated from the French by A. M. Berrett. London: Zed Books, 1988.

Grossman, David. *Sleeping on a Wire: Conversations with Palestinians in Israel*. Translated by Haim Watzman. London: Picador, 1994.

Groueff, Stephane. *Crown of Thorns*. Lanham, Md.: Madison Books, 1987.

Grozev, Kostadin, et al. *1903–2003: 100 Years of Diplomatic Relations Between Bulgaria and the United Sates*. Sofia: Embassy of the United States of America in Bulgaria, 2003.

Haddad, Simon. *The Palestinian Impasse in Lebanon: The Politics of Refugee Integration*. Brighton: Sussex Academic Press, 1988.

Hashavia, Arye. *A History of the Six-Day War*. Tel Aviv: Ledory Publishing House, n.d.

Heikal, Mohamed. *Secret Channels: The Inside Story of Arab-Israeli Peace Negotiations*. London: HarperCollins Publishers, 1996.

Herzog, Chaim. *The Arab-Israeli Wars: War and Peace in the Middle East*. New York: Vintage Books, 1982.

Hillel, Shlomo. *Ruah Kadim*. Jerusalem: 'Idanim, 1985.

Hillenbrand, Carole. *The Crusades: Islamic Perspectives*. New York: Routledge, 2000.

Hiro, Dilip. *Sharing the Promised Land: A Tale of Israelis and Palestinians*. New York: Olive Branch Press, 1999.

Hirsch, Ellen, ed. *Facts About Israel*. Jerusalem: Ahva Press, 1999.

Hirst, David. *The Gun and the Olive Branch: The Roots of Violence in the Middle East*. New York: Thunder's Mouth Press/Nation Books, 2003.

Hroub, Khaled. *Hamas: Political Thought and Practice*. Washington, D.C.: Institute for Palestine Studies, 2000.

Idinopulos, Thomas A. *Weathered by Miracles: A History of Palestine from Bonaparte and Muhammad Ali to Ben-Gurion and the Mufti*. Chicago: Ivan R. Dee, 1998.

Janik, Allan, and Stephen Toulmin. *Wittgenstein's Vienna*. New York: Simon & Schuster, 1973.

Jayyusi, Salma Khadra, ed. *Anthology of Modern Palestinian Literature*. New York: Columbia University Press, 1992.

Kallen, Horace Meyer. *Zionism and World Politics: A Study in History and Social Psychology*. Garden City, N.Y.: Doubleday, Page & Co., 1921.

Kamhi, Rafael Moshe. *Recollections of a Jewish Macedonian Revolutionary*. Sineva, Bulgaria: 2001.

Kanaana, Sharif. *Folk Heritage of Palestine*. Israel: Research Center for Arab Heritage, 1994.

———. *Still on Vacation!: The Eviction of the Palestinians in 1948*. Jerusalem: SHAML—Palestinian Diaspora and Refugee Centre, 2000.

Karmi, Ghada. *In Search of Fatima: A Palestinian Story*. London: Verso, 2002.

Karsh, Efraim. *Fabricating Israeli History: The "New Historians."* London: Frank Cass & Co., 1997.

Khalidi, Rashid. *Palestinian Identity: The Construction of Modern National Consciousness*. New York: Columbia University Press, 1997.

Khalidi, Walid, ed. *Before Their Diaspora: A Photographic History of the Palestinians, 1876–1948*. Washington, D.C.: Institute for Palestine Studies, 1991.

———. *From Haven to Conquest: Readings in Zionism and the Palestine Problem Until 1948*. Beirut: Institute for Palestine Studies, 1971.

————, with Kamal Abdul Fattah, Linda Butler, Sharif S. Elmusa, Ghazi Falah, Albert Glock, Sharif Kanaana, Muhammad Ali Khalidi, and William C. Young. *All That Remains: The Palestinian Villages Occupied and Depopulated by Israel in 1948.* Washington, D.C.: Institute for Palestine Studies, 1992.

Kirkbride, Sir Alec. *From the Wings: Amman Memoirs, 1947–1951.* London: Frank Cass, 1976.

Koen, Albert. *Saving of the Jews in Bulgaria, 1941–1944.* Bulgaria: State Publishing House, 1977.

Kossev, D., H. Hristov, and D. Angelov. *A Short History of Bulgaria.* Translated by Marguerite Alexieva and Nicolai Koledarov. Sofia: Foreign Languages Press, 1963.

Lamm, Zvi. *Youth Takes the Lead: The Inception of Jewish Youth Movements in Europe.* Translated from the Hebrew by Sionah Kronfeld-Honig. Givat Haviva, Israel: Yad Ya'ari, 2004.

Langer, Felicia. *With My Own Eyes.* London: Ithaca Press, 1975.

Lockman, Zachary. *Comrades and Enemies: Arab and Jewish Workers in Palestine, 1906–1948.* Berkeley, Calif.: University of California Press, 1996.

Lowenthal, Marvin, ed. and trans. *The Diaries of Theodor Herzl.* New York: Dial Press, 1956.

Lustick, Ian. *Triumph and Catastrophe: The War of 1948, Israeli Independence, and the Refugee Problem.* New York: Garland Publishing, Inc., 1994.

Maksoud, Clovis (introduction). *Palestine Lives: Interviews with Leaders of the Resistance.* Beirut: Palestine Research Center and Kuawiti Teachers Association, 1973.

Masalha, Nur. *Expulsion of the Palestinians: The Concept of "Transfer" in Zionist Political Thought, 1882–1948.* Washington, D.C.: Institute for Palestine Studies, 1992.

————. *Imperial Israel and the Palestinians: The Politics of Expansion.* London: Pluto Press, 2000.

Mattar, Philip. *The Mufti of Jerusalem.* New York: Columbia University Press, 1988.

Miller, Ylana N. *Government and Society in Rural Palestine, 1920–1948.* Austin, Texas: University of Texas Press, 1985.

Milstein, Uri. *History of Israel's War of Independence, Vol. IV: Out of Crisis Came Decision.* Translated from the Hebrew and edited by Alan Sacks. Lanham, Md.: University Press of America, 1998.

Minchev, Ognyan, Valeri Ratchev, and Marin Lessenski, eds. *Bulgaria for Nato 2002.* Sofia: Open Society Foundation, 2002.

Minns, Amina, and Nadia Hijab. *Citizens Apart: A Portrait of the Palestinians in Israel.* London: I. B. Taurus & Co., 1990.

Morris, Benny. *1948 and After: Israel and the Palestinians.* Oxford: Clarendon Press, 1994.

———. *Israel's Border Wars, 1949–1956: Arab Infiltration, Israeli Retaliation, and the Countdown to the Suez War.* Oxford: Clarendon Press, 1993.

———. *Righteous Victims: A History of the Zionist Arab Conflict, 1881–2001.* New York: Vintage Books, 2001.

———. *The Road to Jerusalem: Glubb Pasha, Palestine and the Jews.* London: I. B. Tauris, 2002.

Musallam, Sami, compiler. *United Nations Resolutions on Palestine, 1947–1972.* Beirut: Institute for Palestine Studies, 1973.

Mutawi, Samir A. *Jordan in the 1967 War.* Cambridge: Cambridge University Press, 1987.

Neff, Donald. *Fallen Pillars: U.S. Policy Towards Palestine and Israel Since 1945.* Washington, D.C.: Institute for Palestine Studies, 1995.

Oren, Michael B. *Six Days of War: June 1967 and the Making of the Modern Middle East.* New York: Ballantine Books, 2003.

Oz, Amos. *In the Land of Israel.* Translated by Maurie Goldberg-Bartura. San Diego, Calif.: Harcourt Brace & Co., 1993.

Pappe, Ilan. *A History of Modern Palestine: One Land, Two Peoples.* Cambridge: Cambridge University Press, 2004.

Patai, Raphael. *The Arab Mind.* New York: Charles Scribner's Sons, 1973.

Pearlman, Moshe. *The Army of Israel.* New York: Philosophical Library, 1950.

Pearlman, Wendy. *Occupied Voices: Stories of Everyday Life from the Second Intifada.* New York: Thunder's Mouth Press/Nation Books, 2003.

Podeh, Elie. *The Arab-Israeli Conflict in Israeli History Textbooks, 1948–2000.* Westport, Conn.: Bergin & Garvey, 2002.

Pryce-Jones, David. *The Face of Defeat: Palestinian Refugees and Guerrillas.* London: Weidenfeld & Nicolson, 1972.

Quigley, John. *Palestine and Israel: A Challenge to Justice.* Durham: Duke University Press, 1990.

Reeve, Simon. *One Day in September: The Full Story of the 1972 Munich Olympic Massacre and Israeli Revenge Operation "Wrath of God."* New York: Arcade Publishing, 2001.

Rogan, Eugene L., and Avi Shlaim, eds. T*he War for Palestine: Rewriting the History of 1948.* Cambridge: Cambridge University Press, 2001.

Ross, Dennis. *The Missing Peace: The Inside Story of the Fight for Middle East Peace.* New York: Farrar, Straus & Giroux, 2004.

Roy, Sara. *The Gaza Strip: The Political Economy of De-Development.* Washington, D.C.: Institute for Palestine Studies, 1995.

Sacco, Joe. *Palestine.* Seattle, Wash.: Fantagraphics Books, 2001.

Said, Edward W. *Out of Place: A Memoir.* New York: Alfred A. Knopf, 1999.

———. *Peace and Its Discontents: Essays on Palestine in the Middle East Peace Process.* New York: Vintage Books, 1995.

———. *Politics of Dispossession: The Struggle for Self-Determination, 1967–1994.* New York: Vintage Books, 1995.

Salti, Ramzi M. *The Native Informant and Other Stories.* Colorado Springs, Colo.: Three Continents Press, 1994.

Samara, Adel, Toby Shelley, Ben Cashdan, et al., contributors. *Palestine: Profile of an Occupation.* London: Zed Books Ltd., 1989.

Sayigh, Yezid. *Armed Struggle and the Search for State: The Palestinian National Movement, 1949–1993.* Oxford: Clarendon Press, 1997.

Schleifer, Abdullah. *The Fall of Jerusalem.* London: Monthly Review Press, 1972.

Segev, Tom. *One Palestine Complete: Jews and Arabs Under the British Mandate.* New York: Metropolitan Books, 1999. Translation copy, 2000.

———. *1949: The First Israelis.* New York: Free Press, 1986.

Shapira, Avraham, ed. *The Seventh Day: Soldiers' Talk About the Six Day War.* London: Andre Deutsch Ltd., 1970.

Shehadeh, Raja. *Strangers in the House: Coming of Age in Occupied Palestine.* South Royalton, Vt.: Steerforth Press, 2002.

Shemesh, Moshe. *The Palestinian Entity 1959–1974: Arab Politics and the PLO.* London: Frank Cass, 1996.

Shlaim, Avi. *The Iron Wall: Israel and the Arab World.* London: Penguin Books, 2000.

———. *War and Peace in the Middle East: A Concise History Revised and Updated.* London: Penguin Books, 1995.

Singer, Howard. *Bring Forth the Mighty Men: On Violence and the Jewish Character.* New York: Funk & Wagnalls, 1969.

Slyomovics, Susan. *The Object of Memory: Arab and Jew Narrate the Palestinian Village.* Philadelphia: University of Pennsylvania Press, 1998.

Sprinzak, Ehud. *Brother Against Brother.* New York: Free Press, 1999.

Stein, Kenneth. *The Land Question in Palestine, 1917–1939.* Chapel Hill, N.C.: University of North Carolina Press, 1984.

Steinberg, Milton. *The Making of the Modern Jew.* Lanham, Md.: University Press of America, 1976.

Swedenburg, Ted. *Memories of Revolt: The 1936–1939 Rebellion and the Palestinian National Past.* Minneapolis, Minn.: University of Minnesota Press, 1995.

Swisher, Clayton E. *The Truth About Camp David: The Untold Story About the Collapse of the Middle East Peace Process.* New York: Nation Books, 2004.

Tamir, Vicki. *Bulgaria and Her Jews: The History of a Dubious Symbiosis.* New York: Sepher-Hermon Press, Inc., for Yeshiva University Press, 1979.

Tavener, L. Ellis. *The Revival of Israel.* London: Hodder & Stoughton, 1961.

Tavin, Eli, and Yonah Alexander. *Psychological Warfare and Propaganda: Irgun Documentation.* Wilmington, Del.: Scholarly Resources Inc., 1982.

Teveth, Shabtai. *The Tanks of Tammuz.* London: Weidenfeld & Nicolson, 1968.

Todorov, Tzvetan. *The Fragility of Goodness: Why Bulgaria's Jews Survived the Holocaust.* Translated from the French by Arthur Denner. Princeton, N.J.: Princeton University Press, 1999.

Tyler, Warwick P. *State Lands and Rural Development in Mandatory Palestine, 1920–1948.* Brighton, U.K.: Sussex Academic Press, 1988.

Vassileva, Boyka. *The Jews in Bulgaria 1944–1952*. Portions translated from the Bulgarian by Polia Alexandrova. Sofia: University Publishing House, St. Kliment Ohridski, 1992.

Yablonka, Hanna. *Survivors of the Holocaust: Israel After the War*. New York: New York University Press, 1999.

Yahya, Adel H. *The Palestinian Refugees, 1948–1998: An Oral History*. Ramallah: Palestinian Association for Cultural Exchange, 1999.

INDEX